THE STEP-BY-STEP
Bar & Bat Mitzvah
PLANNING GUIDE

Avoid Squandering Precious Time and Money, Prevent Guest Disappointment, and Put On a Sensational Bar/Bat Mitzvah

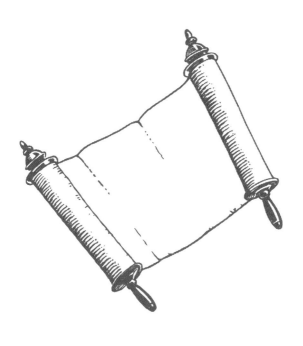

THE STEP-BY-STEP
Bar & Bat
Mitzvah
PLANNING GUIDE

Avoid Squandering Precious Time and Money, Prevent Guest Disappointment, and Put On a Sensational Bar/Bat Mitzvah

BY WENDY WEBER

CONTRIBUTORS:

RABBI MARK SIEDLER
LYNETTA AVERY

WITH FOREWORD BY:

RABBI BRIAN SCHULDENFREI

The Step-by-Step Bar and Bat Mitzvah Planning Guide

Avoid Squandering Precious Time and Money, Prevent Guest Disappointment, and Put On a Sensational Bar/Bat Mitzvah

Author: Wendy Weber
Contributors: Rabbi Mark Siedler, Lynetta Avery, Rabbi Brian Schuldenfrei

Copyright © 2018 by Wendy Weber

Editor: Alana Garrigues

Book Cover Designer: Jessica Richardson

Formatter: Chris Osman

First Publication Date: May 2018

ISBN-13: 978-1986419581

Dedication

We dedicate this book to you.

May you find this tool useful as you plan and execute this important event in your child's life.

May the Bar or Bat Mitzvah that you host

be as inspirational, sensational, and memorable

as you wish it to be.

And may you have the courage to make wise decisions.

Table of Contents

Foreword
By Rabbi Brian Schuldenfrei

For many parents, planning a Bar or Bat Mitzvah is an overwhelming experience. Sometimes, it can be too much!

Without resources or support, parents can feel like the big day is quickly spiraling out of control. For those parents, help is on the way!

Building on her own experiences and lessons learned from planning her daughter's Bat Mitzvah, Wendy offers a comprehensive guide with many practical tips.

Her guide will help you organize, strategize, and arrange all aspects of the upcoming *simcha* (happy occasion). Most importantly, her book will help you feel confident and focus on what is truly important— the blessing of a child embracing their Jewish identity.

Many thanks to you, Wendy, for this invaluable gift!

Chapter 1
Guide Navigation

Who This Guide Is For

This planning guide is meant to help parents and the Bar or Bat Mitzvah teen prepare for the ceremony and celebration. It may also be used by Jewish and non-Jewish guests and by vendors to better understand the traditions behind a Bar and Bat Mitzvah and to navigate expectations.

Parents should read the entire guide.

The Bar or Bat Mitzvah teen should concentrate on Chapter 2 (focus on Mitzvah projects), Chapter 5 (the section on common guest questions) and Chapter 8 (the ceremony).

Both Jewish and non-Jewish guests may wish to familiarize themselves with Chapter 5 (guest FAQs), Chapter 8 (the ceremony), and the sections about Jewish traditions and Kosher law in Chapter 11.

Tip

Parents and the Bar or Bat Mitzvah teen should read the same sections carefully to be aware of the guests' experience. Non-Jewish guests may be experiencing their first Bar/Bat Mitzvah and wonder about meaning and guest protocol. These sections will help anticipate questions.

The timetables and celebratory information in this book, found in Chapters 4 and 11, will help vendors and hired professionals understand how their services fit into the event, and avoid potential pitfalls.

NOTE: The terms Bar and Bat Mitzvah are used in two different ways in the Jewish tradition. Sometimes they refer to the ceremony of becoming a Jewish adult. Other times, the words refer to the teens themselves. Bar Mitzvah refers to a Bar Mitzvah boy and Bat Mitzvah refers to a Bat Mitzvah girl. This planning guide uses the term both ways. The plural term B'nai Mitzvah refers to groups of Bar and Bat Mitzvah boys and girls.

Why We Wrote This Guide

We decided to write this book after numerous people shared with us their terrible experiences attending a Bar or Bat Mitzvah. We heard a lot of negative feedback, ranging from confusion to complaints.

Questions and Concerns

- "The noise level was so loud that it hurt my ears and I had to leave early."

- "I had to pay for my drinks."

- "I felt uncomfortable not knowing what was going on."

- "The dance floor was so small that I got stepped on multiple times." (Ouch!)

- "That Bar Mitzvah ceremony was long and torturous."

- "I was left out and felt like an outsider."

- "I didn't know what to wear."

- "I didn't know the service would be mostly in Hebrew, which I don't understand."

- "I didn't know what kind of gift to buy or how much money to send."

- "How will I make it through another Bar or Bat Mitzvah?"

This planning guide will help you simplify planning and production, make the event special for Jewish and non-Jewish friends alike, and make smart use of your Bar or Bat Mitzvah dollars. Our goal is to help you create an unforgettable experience that will be remembered fondly by all.

There were many online resources that I found helpful as I went through the personal journey of planning my daughter's Bat Mitzvah, but there was no comprehensive guide. I found bits of information scattered here and there, and it took a lot of effort to piece it all together. There were a handful of books on Amazon, but again, many were missing valuable information and didn't quite target what I needed as far as a comprehensive guideline with clear steps to follow.

This planning guide aims to fill that gap. Our intent is to support you throughout the process and alleviate stress, by providing concrete ideas and suggestions to move you forward and make your event a success.

We offer a comprehensive understanding of the Mitzvah process, from early planning to the ceremony, and through the reception and celebratory portion of the Bar or Bat Mitzvah.

Chapter 2
What Is a Bar or Bat Mitzvah?

In the olden days of much shorter lifespans, a Bar Mitzvah (thirteen-year-old boy) became a Jewish adult. Literally a *Son of the Commandments*, he transitioned from childhood and was considered fully responsible for his actions. The Bar Mitzvah marked his spiritual and moral development, and he could now participate fully in synagogue life. The rite of passage was marked with the Bar Mitzvah publicly reading the Torah and *Haftarah* (reading from the Book of Prophets) in Hebrew for the first time.

In some synagogues, the Bar Mitzvah also led part of the services and even performed the *D'var Torah* (sermon). *D'var Torah*, literally a "Word of Torah" and shows the congregation that the celebrant has reached a certain level of intellectual and spiritual maturity by thoughtfully delving into the meaning and background of the Torah portion for that day.

In the last century, girls were allowed to participate in a Bat Mitzvah ceremony in Conservative, Reform and some liberal Orthodox synagogues. Depending on the synagogue, girls become a Bat Mitzvah at thirteen years old although there are some synagogues where a girl is considered a Bat Mitzvah at the age of twelve. Age may fluctuate between synagogues and movements, since in some stricter Orthodox circles, girls may not have a traditional Bat Mitzvah ceremony at all.

Tikkun Olam Mitzvah Projects

The Bar or Bat Mitzvah services mark an important shift in the young teen's life. The youth's primary focus begins to transition from personal concerns (e.g., school, sports, friends, social activities) to spiritual and societal considerations—how they can contribute to the Jewish community, Israel and the world at large. This broadened scope is called *Tikkun Olam*, literally "repairing the world." It is achieved through volunteering, social justice work, and philanthropy.

Many Bar and Bat Mitzvah demonstrate this entry into Jewish adulthood by undertaking a Mitzvah project, raising money or collecting items to support a charity and cause that means something to them.

The chosen Mitzvah project can be integrated into speeches, themes, and centerpieces, and be used as a communication tool as your Mitzvah teen sets project goals and reaches out to guests to participate. It is a good way to add a meaningful connection between guests and the Bar or Bat Mitzvah.

I recently attended one Bar Mitzvah where the teen asked guests to donate musical instruments and related musical items. He set up a box to drop them off in the sanctuary lobby. The Bar Mitzvah's *Tikkun Olam* project was to improve musical access for underprivileged kids.

I have also seen Mitzvah project requests for used books, sports equipment, clothing, toys, and blankets. These items were then donated to various American and Israeli charities.

Charitable Donations

Instead of collecting material items, your teen may choose to make a financial contribution, donating a portion of monetary Bar and Bat Mitzvah gifts to charitable organizations.

Encourage autonomy and adult decision-making by allowing them to choose the charity that has special meaning in their heart.

Organizations to Consider

If your teen doesn't have a charity or cause in mind, consider cancer research, animal sanctuaries, programs to help the homeless and less fortunate in our midst, or organizations that save the environment.

I'd like to share four organizations that I would highly recommend. These charities do good work and have successfully helped many people and animals through their outreach programs.

Holy Land Cats

If you want to donate to a great Israeli organization, I recommend Holy Land Cats in Jerusalem. This group rescues homeless kittens and cats wandering the streets, susceptible to disease, lack of food, and injury. If you would like to support this cause, please reach out to Anna Saul at tovasaul@yahoo.com.

Neve College for Women

Yeshiva and Colleges in Israel are great organizations to donate to. One college that has helped numerous Israeli and American girls is Neve College for Women in Jerusalem. You can donate to them on their website at nevey.org or contact Ellen Clyman at EllenClyman@nevey.org.

World Animal Protection

This organization sets up bear sanctuaries in Pakistan that focus on rescuing and housing bears used for bear baiting, a cruel practice that forces bears to fight for entertainment. Cubs are taken from their mothers, their teeth and claws removed. They are then put into a ring, tied to a short rope, where they must face trained fighting dogs. Many of the bears lose their eyesight and cannot fend for themselves.

The bear sanctuary's main purpose is to save these traumatized bears. The former captives who still have the vision are healed and returned into the wild, while blind bears remain at the sanctuary for the rest of their lives.

Please consider donating to this worthy cause at www.worldanimalprotection.org. The full link to support the bears and other animals in danger can be found in the resources section at the back of this book.

The Nature Conservancy

This environmental organization has conservation projects in more than 72 countries, including all of the 50 United States. They focus on land and water conservation projects and in doing so protect nature, preserve wildlife and save endangered species. More information can be found on their website at www.nature.org.

See Mitzvah Bowl for More

For additional ideas, visit the Mitzvah Bowl website at www.themitzvahbowl.com.

Chapter 3
Spiritual Focus
and Consistency

Before we get into the details of Bar or Bat Mitzvah planning, a gentle reminder: It is important to maintain a spiritual connection between the ceremony (the traditional part of the Bar or Bat Mitzvah which occurs on Saturday morning) and the *simcha* (some sort of celebration—may vary from a luncheon to a formal evening event).

Even though my daughter's Bat Mitzvah was a few years ago, friends and family approach me to this day and remark that was the best celebration they have ever been to. I think this is in large part due to the care we took to align the ceremony and the celebration spiritually, and the thought we gave to our guests' experience. It is my hope that this planning guide inspires you to give deep thought and consideration to both.

Celebration Versus Party

You will notice that throughout the planning guide I use the English translation of the Hebrew *simcha*, meaning "a joyous occasion, a celebration" rather than party. This is done on purpose. In my view, there is a significant difference between a party and a celebration.

The word "party" is void of spiritual connection and the purpose behind the Bar or Bat Mitzvah. The entire event should reflect the emotional, moral, and spiritual development of the teen.

The term "celebration," which more closely matches the Hebrew term *simcha*, acknowledges the Bar or Bat Mitzvah's accomplishment and the transition into adulthood. They have entered into a life-long partnership with G-d and vow to take on more responsibility and adhere to Torah laws.

These Torah laws and principles should be carefully considered when planning the sacred Bar or Bat Mitzvah celebration. The first event (the ceremony) and the second event (the celebration) must be connected and maintain a reverent, respectful atmosphere. Otherwise, guests may feel bewildered and confused as to why the ceremony had such meaning, while the celebration veered from the precepts emphasized earlier in the day.

The goal when planning the weekend should be to bridge the gap between the ceremony and the celebration so that it is fluid and has a sense of unity and connection.

The Spiritual Importance and Meaning

I have been to countless parties that I left early due to loud music and other disturbing issues. As I looked at the other guests' faces, all I could see was boredom, disgust, and disillusionment.

Why is it so important to host a memorable Bar or Bat Mitzvah?

I believe we have an obligation to the Jewish and non-Jewish community to set a good example of the true spiritual meaning of the B'nai Mitzvah. This may be a non-Jew's only opportunity for a close-up encounter with Judaism, so it is important that we put our best foot forward.

You want to make your child's Bar or Bat Mitzvah special for everyone involved.

Your young adult has spent anywhere from one to four years preparing for this event. For the first time in a Bar or Bat

Mitzvah's life, they will experience the blessing of their Jewish and non-Jewish community gathering around to celebrate them. It would be a mistake to take the day lightly. A Jewish child will remember their Bar or Bat Mitzvah as the most significant Jewish experience of their life, up until their wedding day.

With careful planning, you can avoid turning this special day into the Groundhog Day of B'nai Mitzvot and make sure the memories made that day are good ones, not bad.

Themes: A Word of Caution

Themes are popular. They make it easy to plan invitations, entertainment, and decorations. They also run the risk of overpowering the significance of the day by diverting the attention from a religious event to a party atmosphere.

For that reason, we chose not to implement a theme. Still, my daughter's celebration was fantastic and remarkably successful, and we received wonderful feedback in the form of verbal and written communication from guests, who said they had an amazing time.

Keep in mind that a Mitzvah already has a built-in theme— your teenager coming of age. They are stepping into "adulthood," taking on additional responsibilities in observance of and adherence to religious law and guidelines and becoming a responsible member of the community.

Do we really need to layer another theme on top of the Mitzvah to dilute the religious significance? I don't think so.

Thinking back to when I was a child celebrating my Bat Mitzvah and attending friends' Bar and Bat Mitzvahs, no one had a theme.

I find an authentic, traditional Mitzvah timeless. And it can still be beautiful, tasteful, and lots of fun!

That said, if you really have your heart set on a theme to plan within defined parameters, there are plenty of resources out there.

The first step would be to check in with your child to see what theme they prefer. You might want to pick one of their favorite activities and build a personal theme around that, or you can choose a theme that closely ties in with your child's Mitzvah project.

If nothing comes to mind immediately, and you still want to do a theme, the website Beaucoup (www.beau-coup.com) covers themes tastefully. You can find a link directly to Bar and Bat Mitzvah themes in the resources section at the back of this book.

Chapter 4
Timeline: The Two Year Checklist

This chapter outlines major planning and decision making that you should be aware of as you work toward the Bar or Bat Mitzvah and explains those steps. The timetables start two years out. If you are less than two years out from the event, don't worry. Read through the timetables, check off what has already been done, and then make an action plan to get caught up.

Most of the items on the to-do list are explained in much greater detail in the chapters that follow. Use this guide as a general compass or map, so that you are aware of what's to come.

Check the appendices for a timeline without the extra discussion include in this chapter. Use that to quickly and easily keep track of your progress.

24 Months Before the Event

- ☐ Lock in Your Date

- ☐ Ask About Synagogue Requirements

- ☐ Begin Bar/Bat Mitzvah Preparation

- ☐ Estimate Number of Guests

- ☐ Determine Budget and Event Parameters (Day, Evening, Formal, Luncheon, etc.)

- ☐ Book a Venue

Lock in Your Date

Your child's Bat or Bar Mitzvah will be on or after the child's thirteenth birthday (for a boy) or twelfth birthday (for a girl). This may fluctuate between religious movements and synagogue practices.

To get an approximate date, go to chabad.org and search for "Bar (or Bat) Mitzvah Calendar." Right at the top of the search terms, you should find a link labeled tools, with the headline "Bar/Bat Mitzvah Date Calendar." Click on it, and the free online calculator will give you an idea of when your child will celebrate and the Torah portion that may be read on that day. The online calendar should not be considered the authority on the matter. Always confirm readings and Bar or Bat Mitzvah dates with your synagogue.

Practices vary among synagogues, but usually, the date assigned is as close as possible to your child's Hebrew birthday.

Be aware that date assignments can be scheduled two to three years in advance, so give the synagogue plenty of notice if you have a conflict with the date assigned. The Bar or Bat Mitzvah is sometimes booked for a weekday. In that case, you may wish to ask if it is possible to move it forward to the next *Shabbat*.

Remember, you can make a request, but your synagogue may be balancing your child's date request with a full calendar. Ultimately, the date of the Bar or Bat Mitzvah will be selected according to the synagogue's availability.

We were fortunate that our date change request was granted. Our synagogue had originally scheduled my daughter's Bat Mitzvah for the weekend of Halloween. We were concerned about weather and the holiday. We knew many kids would want to go trick-or-treating that same day. When we reached out to the synagogue to express our concerns, they graciously assigned a summer date that was more favorable.

Ask About Synagogue Requirements

As you are working with the synagogue or temple on your date, the synagogue will generally provide you with guidelines and requirements that will help aid you through the process of preparing for your child's Bar Mitzvah. Your child typically would be enrolled in Hebrew School and begin the preparation process around one to two years before their Bar or Bat Mitzvah. The guidelines that the synagogue will provide typically cover: ceremony expectations, the selecting of Torah honors such as *Aliyot* and other ceremonial tasks, financial obligations including all Bar or Bat Mitzvah fees and catering costs, clergy meeting schedules, and mandatory service attendance requirements.

We've outlined major traditions associated with most ceremonies in Chapter 8, but you'll need to work closely with your synagogue to gain an understanding of their customs and practices.

Begin Bar/Bat Mitzvah Preparation

In most cases, your child probably already attends Hebrew school, and the synagogue will automatically set up steps to begin the process of Bar or Bat Mitzvah preparation. These steps might include individual tutoring where they will work with a teacher, Cantor or Rabbi.

During the preparation process, your child will learn how to chant their Torah portion and other relevant prayers related to the service. Check with your synagogue for a list of the required prayers your child must be proficient at. They will also work on their speech and explore and evaluate the meaning of their Torah portion. In some synagogues, children attend a group class with other kids their age to gain further knowledge of Hebrew and other Jewish concepts.

Estimate Number of Guests

Once you have a firm date for the Bar or Bat Mitzvah, estimate the number of guests you'll expect to have. Make a list of family, friends, and important people in your Bar or Bat Mitzvah's life. Think of friends, co-workers, relatives, mentors, and people who have supported your family throughout the years.

Check in with your child to see whom they would like on the invitation list and be sure to add those people important in your child's life. Also, the synagogue may have an optional policy where you are encouraged you to invite all of the students in your child's Hebrew class to avoid anyone from feeling excluded.

Determine Budget and Event Parameters

Your budget will have a major impact on the type of celebration you will host, including the location and time of day.

Read through Chapter 6 carefully for a list of budget items and celebration options to fit any budget. Expenses do add up, so you may want to start saving earlier rather than later to spread out the cost of the Mitzvah weekend.

If your budget is on the lower end and you choose to host an intimate celebration to fit your budget, revisit your guest list to make sure that close family and friends will be included in the count. Make sure they are on the invitation list to avoid dealing with hurt feelings and fallouts later on.

Book a Venue

The location of your celebration will determine the atmosphere of the event. You will need to have an approximate guest list count in mind to determine the size of the space you will need. With that in mind, start researching venues and hotels, and make appointments with venue coordinators to tour the space and learn about pricing and other services they offer.

Be aware of minimum fees so that you are sure to secure a venue that fit within your budget.

Sign a contract and book the venue as soon as you have found the right fit for your celebration. It may seem early, but you don't want to lose out on your preferred location by waiting too long, only to find out your date has been taken by a wedding reception or milestone birthday party.

For more information on booking a venue, including a list of several questions to ask the venue coordinator while you research, see Chapter 10.

18 Months Before the Event

- ☐ Research and Select: Band, DJ, Photographer, Videographer, Florist, Entertainers
- ☐ Research, Interview, Select Caterer(s)
- ☐ Consider Hiring an Event Planner

Research and Select Band, DJ, Photographer, Videographer, Florist, Entertainers

This is the time to research and select all of your helpers—the caterer, bands, DJs, photographers, videographers and other entertainers. You want to speak with them as early as possible to lock in dates, especially if you'll be hosting a Bar or Bat Mitzvah in the summer months. These vendors also provide entertainment for weddings, conferences, sweet sixteen parties, quincañeras, anniversaries, and graduation parties. You will not want to miss out on high-quality service just because someone else scooped up your preferred vendor first.

Don't know where to start looking? You can join Bar Mitzvah Facebook groups in your region to ask questions and find the best entertainment and other ideas for your Mitzvah. You can also ask around to find out who friends and family recommend, or you can spend hours doing online research, but I suggest that you turn to the people who throw events all the time—venue coordinators and event planners.

Hotels and event venues have lists of the best bands, DJs, florists, photographers, videographers and other entertainers (e.g., magicians, jugglers, caricature artists, etc.). Ask your favorite local hotels for referrals. They'll tell you who offers great service with a proven track record—and maybe even whom to avoid.

Once you start reaching out and find entertainers and vendors that you like, ask them if they have any additional recommendations for other service providers. Vendors often work together or run in the same circles and therefore bump into each other at events, so they know whom to trust. Vendors with a history of outstanding entertainment know people, so use their lists of preferred partners to help you.

How can you tell you're speaking with a quality service provider? Ask for references, but don't forget to investigate on your own. Vendors usually maintain websites and social media pages with video footage of past events. Watch those videos and pay close attention to the guests. If videos show happy, engaged, upbeat guests having a great time, you know they are doing something right. However, if guests look bored, move on to the next vendor option.

Research, Interview, and Select Caterer(s)

Read through Chapters 8 and 11 carefully before reaching out to any caterer. You may find that you need to hire and work with more than one caterer for all of the weekend's events. You may also find that you do not need to hire a caterer at all, depending on your celebration venue and your synagogue's policies.

In most synagogues, Friday evening and Saturday morning food service will be mandatory, and you'll also need to provide meals for guests at your celebration.

Some synagogue, hotel, and event venue contracts include clauses that require in-house catering or only allow you to work with a limited selection of pre-approved vendors. If you're not sure, ask. If there is a no-outside-catering policy, you will be expected to abide by it.

Even if you are limited by your catering choices, it is a good idea to meet with the venue or pre-approved caterers to get an idea of cost and menu options. Your synagogue office can also provide you with menus and pricing lists for the Friday evening and Saturday morning meals.

In addition to the major events surrounding the Bar or Bat Mitzvah, you may want to host and cater a Friday dinner and/ or Sunday morning brunch in your home for out-of-town guests.

Consider Hiring an Event Planner

You may find it's easier to manage everything if you work with an event planner. If you do, keep in mind that you can use the event planner for part or all of the entertainment and logistical planning for the celebration. Event planners are there to help you stay organized and on task, plan a cohesive weekend; they can also secure top entertainment. Again, ask hotel or venue for a list of the best event planners.

We worked with an event planner to book some of my daughter's Bat Mitzvah entertainment, including the photographer, videographer, magician, and caricature artist, but we chose to book the band ourselves.

One advantage to hiring an event planner is that they have endless resources of entertainers, and can help you manage challenges if anything goes awry. For example, if the vendor that you hired (say a balloon artist) is unavailable due to an illness or emergency, your event planner would easily be able to call in a replacement. This alone takes much of the pressure off the host/hostess.

If you prefer to think about the big picture and let someone else handle the details, I highly recommend the event planner option. You still have the final say on any decision or contract, but you don't have to coordinate all of the logistics. There is less to worry about from the host's perspective.

If you do choose to hire an event planner for only a portion of the celebration, good communication will be the key to a successful event. Set expectations and key responsibilities early.

12 Months Before the Event

- ☐ Choose Hotel(s) for Out-of-Town Guests
- ☐ Support Bar/Bat Mitzvah's Torah Studies and Check on Progress
- ☐ Begin Work on Custom Centerpieces, Flowers and/or Balloon Decorations
- ☐ Plan Invitations

- ☐ Mail Save the Date Cards

- ☐ Order *Tallit*, *Kippot*

- ☐ Plan Theme (*optional*)

- ☐ Book Tables for Additional Meals (e.g., Sunday Brunch)

Choose Hotel(s) for Out-of-Town Guests

Booking hotel blocks for out-of-town guests is optional. If you know that a large constituency will fly in and want to stay together in the same hotel to mingle before and after the event, socialize and eat together the rest of the weekend, a hotel block is a good idea.

If out-of-town guests do not know each other or have widely varying budgets, consider alternative methods to ease their hotel selection, without worrying about the responsibility of paying for unsold hotel rooms.

The Knot, a website usually used for wedding planning, has good information about hotel room blocks. We've included a direct link in the resources section at the back of this book.

We opted not to block rooms since we didn't know exactly how many out-of-town guests planned to attend, and whether those who did would all want to stay at the same hotel.

Instead, we gave guests three hotel options, listed on the back of save the date card. All three hotels were located within walking distance of the celebration, and they were priced from inexpensive to luxurious. That gave guests options based on their budget and comfort level while allowing them to stay close to the event. Guests who are unfamiliar with the area will especially appreciate your efforts to recommend a handful of hotels located near your venue.

Tip

Ask hotels if they can offer discounts or coupon codes for your guests, even if you do not plan to book a hotel block.

All three of the hotel listings we shared included discount codes, ranging from ten to fifteen percent off normal rates.

That way, we were able to save our guests money and the headache of sifting through dozens of hotel ratings. At the same time, we didn't have to sign another contract, and we avoided penalties associated with blocking rooms that don't get booked.

If you do decide to block rooms, make sure you negotiate guest rates and amenities, as well as terms and penalties concerning unsold rooms. If the hotel is not willing to negotiate, I suggest you contact another hotel more willing to work with you or opt out room blocks altogether.

Support Bar/Bat Mitzvah's Torah Studies and Check on Progress

Torah preparation generally occurs at twelve months out (or longer). Your synagogue will provide a schedule of recurring meetings with the Cantor and Rabbi to ensure your child is making progress.

Most synagogues host special B'nai Mitzvah preparation classes where students whose Bar or Bat Mitzvahs fall around the same time will receive weekly instruction and individual tutorials.

In addition, many synagogues require the Bar or Bat Mitzvah and their parents to attend a specific number of Shabbat morning services. This helps the parents and child gain a better understanding of the importance of the rituals and get comfortable with the service structure and meaning of the prayers.

Check with your synagogue now to familiarize yourself with the required schedule. Failure to meet synagogue requirements may result in postponement or cancellation of your child's Bar or Bat Mitzvah service, so make it a priority to follow the guidelines.

Begin Work on Custom Centerpieces, Flowers, and/or Balloon Decorations

Even though the event is a year away, this is the time to plan the décor and begin to prepare any custom centerpieces.

If you haven't already hired a florist and plan to have professionally arranged flowers at the event, finish gathering quotes for centerpieces and/or balloon decorations now, and look at photos for inspiration. Select flowers that will be in season and readily available, and ask your florist for quotes.

If you're looking for a unique centerpiece, see Chapter 11 for alternatives to flowers. My daughter and I made custom centerpieces for her Bat Mitzvah. We will always hold special memories of planning and crafting them together.

Plan Invitations

Consider hiring an invitation specialist to help you navigate the complexities of paper invitations—from what to include and what to avoid, to the best paper and style to complement your event.

Even though hiring a professional will be more expensive than going online and doing it yourself, a guide can offer peace of mind, especially when it comes to knowing what should be included in the invitation. There is a milieu of traditions to be aware of, and knowing how modern technology fits into age-old tradition can be tricky. Invitation specialists are aware of traditions and trends and can help you figure out the best way to communicate the event and set the tone.

There are many styles, colors, themes, fonts, and papers to choose from and without a helping hand, it can feel overwhelming. An invitation specialist can guide you toward the right options for you.

I appreciated the ability to physically see and touch invitation samples before I placed an order. I wanted to know the quality of the paper and printing before a box full of invitations arrived at the door. That is not possible with an online order.

Tip

Be aware that the invitation specialists may try to upsell you with extras such as leaflets and inserts, embossing, monograms, and so on. These are lovely, but not necessary. If you're on a tight budget, stick to the four basics: envelope, invitation, RSVP card, and save the date card.

For more detailed information about invitations and printed material, see Chapter 7. While you won't mail invitations until closer to the event, it takes time to select the style and wording that works for you, and you'll need to order invitations months before mailing them.

Mail Save the Date Cards

Once your guest list is complete, send out save the date cards. These cards are less formal and informative than the invitation, but they let friends and family know that they are on your guest list.

The save the date cards should include the date, time, and location of the ceremony and celebration, as well as hotel information for out-of-town guests. You may also wish to include a link to a personalized Mitzvah website, which should be updated as the date gets closer with additional information such as the *Tikkun Olam* projects (if you plan on involving your guests with this), the weekend's events, and messages from the Bar or Bat Mitzvah.

A save the date card allows guests to reserve the date or weekend for your big celebration so that they can plan accordingly. Save the dates are especially important for out-of-town guests who will make flight and hotel arrangements, but also appreciated by local guests who will want to avoid conflicts such as weekend travel or tickets to theater or sporting events.

Order *Tallit, Kippot*

Order a *tallit* (prayer shawl) for the Bar or Bat Mitzvah child and parents and any family member who plans on being on the *Bimah* (altar). Synagogues generally require anyone who is called up for an *Aliyah* (Torah reading) or to otherwise participate on the *Bimah* (altar) to wear a *tallit*. Boys and men must also wear a *kippah* (head covering, also known as a *yarmulke*) in most synagogues.

Make sure your *tallitot* (plural of *tallit*) meet synagogue standards. Be aware that buying a *tallit* through Amazon is not advised. You might end up with a messianic *tallit* that is not up to standards.

Instead, look for your family's *tallitot* in person. Temple gift shops typically stock a good selection of high-quality *tallitot*. Big cities with an abundance of Judaica stores in Orthodox neighborhoods also sell *tallitot*. Finally, if you plan to go to Israel before the Mitzvah, there are plenty of stores in Jerusalem and other cities that sell them.

Kippot (yarmulkes, or head coverings) can be ordered online. We used kippah.com since they had an extensive variety of fabrics and styles. If you have decided to go with a reception theme, you can order theme-based *kippot* for the ceremony.

When deciding how many to order, consider that usually about half of the guests are male and will need one. Also, remember that not all of your reception guests will attend the ceremony. Some opt to participate in the celebration only.

The best approach when ordering may be "less is more," in order to avoid an abundance of extras to take home. We learned that lesson the hard way. Out of our pool of 150 guests, we had about 25 *kippot* left over. We had ordered 90.

Of course, it is worth noting that this was for my daughter's Bat Mitzvah. A Bar Mitzvah child may have more male guests, in which case our order could have been closer to what was needed.

Plan Theme (*optional*)

If you do decide to incorporate a reception theme, it's time to start planning details—how the theme will be conveyed through food, activities, and decorations. Any theme should be discussed with an invitation specialist so that he or she can integrate this into all of the communications that you order.

For more thoughts on a theme, review Chapter 3. I recommend against it for several reasons that I outline there, but some families find it very helpful in planning the event. If you choose to have a theme, I suggest you might consider tasteful ways to incorporate this into the *Tikkun Olam* Mitzvah project.

Make Reservations for Additional Meals *(optional)*

If you expect a large number of out-of-town guests or local family and close friends who would like to attend a Friday night Shabbat dinner and/or Sunday brunch, make arrangements with a hotel or restaurant to reserve a room. There is usually a minimum charge, and you may be asked to make a down payment to secure the space.

If your guest count is smaller—around a couple dozen or less—you can make table reservations instead, with no upfront costs or minimum order. We had around 25 people attending brunch, so we booked two different tables at the restaurant where we hosted it. Ask the restaurant if there is a maximum number of people per table, and then book the number of tables accordingly.

Be sure to communicate to the restaurant who will pay, so that the wait staff doesn't worry about splitting up a check or giving it to the wrong person—and be aware that the gratuity will likely be included on the bill. This is typically an expense that that host/hostess should cover, so it is important that the bill go to the correct person.

Feel free to get creative with dinner and brunch seating and location. If you'd rather not go to a restaurant, a more intimate and less expensive option may be to host an informal gathering at your home.

We wanted to save most of our precious dollars for the reception, but also avoid the stress of preparing our home for guests in the middle of a busy weekend. By splitting the reservation into two tables, we were able to save a considerable amount of money compared to reserving a private room.

If you are on a tight budget, know that these extra meals are optional. Out-of-town guests may like to have a morning to themselves to sleep in or explore the town, so don't feel pressured to host all meals.

6 Months Before the Event

- ☐ Select Guest Book or Sign-In Board (*optional*)

- ☐ Order Party Favors (*optional*)

- ☐ Write Parent and Teen Speeches

- ☐ Work on Celebration Slideshow (*optional*)

- ☐ Start Shopping for Clothes

- ☐ Select Guest Book or Sign-In Board (*optional*)

If you'd like to have a guest book or special sign-in board or poster at the event, order them ahead of time. The guest book makes for a wonderful memory for years to come, filled with well wishes and loved ones' signatures.

We opted not to include a guest book or sign-in board this since our photographs and videos acted as mementos, but it is a nice touch.

Order Party Favors (*optional*)

If you're going to order party favors, again, this is the time to order them. Party favors come in all shapes and sizes, and there are endless possibilities. Party favors are given out at the reception for guests to take home by guests as souvenirs.

One of the best favors we received at a Bar Mitzvah was a cell phone charger. High tech gadgets can be an innovative party favor. Photo coasters, personalized Mitzvah tea bags, custom colored fortune cookies are all great ideas. My personal favorite is personalized light up cups that can be found at www. cool-party-favors.com.

We opted out of party favors, since our entertainment included a caricature artist and a hat making station, so it came with built-in souvenirs. In addition, one guest from each table was the lucky recipient of a stunning centerpiece.

Write Parent and Teen Speeches

Parent and teen speeches to be used in the ceremony usually have to be approved by the Rabbi, so reach out to the clergy at your local synagogue and set up a time to meet and make sure the speech is on the right track.

Sample parent and teen speeches, as well as guidelines to write them, are included in Chapter 8.

Work on Celebration Slideshow *(optional)*

Look through old photos and videos and begin to select the ones you want to include in your slideshow and video montages. Order a projector and screen online.

Start Shopping for Clothes

The shopping process can be surprisingly time-consuming, and I recommend doing it early to avoid interfering with the busy details that come up closer to the date of the Mitzvah.

Remember you'll need two sets of clothes, shoes, and accessories for each family member: one set for the ceremony and one set for the celebration.

I recommend that you buy parents' clothes and shoes now, and have a tailor make adjustments later if necessary. You may want to hold off on buying the Bar or Bat Mitzvah and siblings' clothing and shoes until closer to the date, especially if they haven't finished growing, but have them try on dresses and suits now to choose favorite styles and colors.

If you visit a dress shop that specializes in clothing for formal events such as weddings, there will be catalogs and samples of each dress or suit in many sizes and colors, just to try on, but purchases will be special ordered. They can take six to twelve weeks to arrive.

For children who are still growing, order clothes a size up and then have them professionally tailored closer to the event, or tell the store the style you like, and check in three to four months before the Bar or Bat Mitzvah to complete the order. Formal dress shops will keep records of client preferences for easy ordering.

Keep clothes classy and consistent with the goals and values reinforced at the ceremony.

During the ceremony, the Bar or Bat Mitzvah is making a commitment, or vow, to adhere to Torah laws. Those laws include modesty and sanctity or the state of being holy. Risqué or indecent clothing conveys the opposite message and is particularly inappropriate for the event.

Invest in shoes and accessories (such as necklaces, earrings, and watches) that are tasteful. Keep in mind that you will spend many hours on your feet at the reception, dancing and circulating to speak with visitors, so I recommend comfortable shoes from a ballroom dance store to prevent blisters and foot cramps.

We splurged on shoes, and went to a dance store in Los Angeles that sells to celebrity clients on "Dancing with the Stars." The comfort was well worth the expense.

3 Months Before the Event

☐ Finalize Guest List and Confirm Missing Addresses for Invitations

- ☐ Plan Table Seating

- ☐ Finalize Catering Menu for Celebration

- ☐ Select Hotel Room Gifts for Out-of-Town Guests (*optional*)

- ☐ Write a Song Playlist: Include Songs for Candle Lighting Ceremony

- ☐ Select Honorees for *Aliyot*, Torah Tasks, and Gift Presentations

- ☐ Make Hair Stylist, Pedicure, Manicure Appointments

Finalize Guest List and Confirm Missing Addresses for Invitations

Finalize the guest list. Now is the time to get into the details of the guest experience. You've already sent your save the date cards, so make sure you still have current addresses for all of those guests. You may have connected with other guests since the save the dates were mailed. Be sure to add those addresses, so that you will be ready to send the invitations out in a few weeks.

If you are printing address labels, print them out a couple of weeks before you mail invitations to avoid any hiccups with printing issues. If you're writing them by hand or doing calligraphy, you should have the envelopes ready to go. It's always wise to have a few more envelopes than invitations, in case you make a mistake.

Plan Table Seating

Strategize table seating using your guest list. Note that there are often last-minute changes to the guest list—both additions and removals—all the way up until the day before the event. Take this in stride.

You have more flexibility and less stress around the guest list if you choose to print your own table seating cards. This way you can avoid the hassle of calling the printer and ordering new cards when you have to rearrange guests at the last minute. I cover more about that in Chapter 9.

We had a few guests invite themselves at the last minute. I was happy to include them. I felt the more the merrier! Plus, it was easy to print the additional table seating cards at home, and their meals helped us reach the venue's minimum for catering costs.

Finalize Catering Menu for Celebration

If you haven't already, work with your celebration caterer (venue or outside caterer) to finalize the menu. Narrow entrées down to three options for guests and select appetizers and desserts. Invitations will be sent out next month, and guest entrée options will be included on RSVP cards or a Mitzvah website.

You will give your caterer a final headcount closer to the date of the celebration, but the menu should be nailed down now.

Select Hotel Room Gifts for Out-of-Town Guests (*optional*)

Hotel gifts for out-of-towners provide a thoughtful touch. This is something that is always appreciated but can be tastefully skipped for the more budget conscious among you. There is also a cost in terms of time and energy, selecting the products to include, and delivering the gift bags to the guests' hotels ahead of the weekend.

If you'd like to put a gift together, there are great resources and ideas online. Just run a search for "hotel guest gift bags," or think about what you'd like if you were visiting. There may be a special food unique to your area, or an item that could help your guests rest and enjoy their time in the hotel or outdoors aside from the Bar or Bat Mitzvah activities.

Tip

Negotiate the delivery cost of the gift bag to the room with the hotel(s).

This was an area where we decided to save time and money. We opted out of gift bags, feeling like our to-do list had already reached the limits of what we could accomplish. Remember that it is okay to sometimes say no to extra tasks.

Write a Song Playlist: Include Candle Lighting Ceremony

Collaborate with your band or DJ on a playlist for the celebration. You don't need to decide on every song, but let the band or DJ know if there are any special songs you want to be sure are included.

If you plan to include a candle lighting ceremony at the reception, you will also need a list of songs to be played as each candle is lit. Read more about the meaning and purpose behind a candle lighting ceremony in Chapter 11.

Select Honorees for *Aliyot*, Torah Tasks, and Gift Presentations

Choose the honored guests that you'd like to read the *Aliyot* (blessings on the Torah reading) and make sure they will be able to say the appropriate blessings in Hebrew. More details on the *Aliyot* can be found in Chapter 8, including transliteration of the blessings. YouTube can help with pronunciation.

Multiple emails may be required between you and the *Aliyot* readers since you will need to gather information such as their Hebrew names and their parents' Hebrew names.

Keep in mind that the requirement to be called up to *Aliyah* in both a Conservative and Orthodox Synagogue is that the person be Jewish. This may be true in a Reform Synagogue as well. Be sure to check with your synagogue so that you know the policy before making your selection.

In addition to readers, you will need a few guests to come up to the *Bimah* (altar) and open and close the ark as well as the *Parochet* (curtain).

Be aware that the Bar or Bat Mitzvah will receive gifts during the ceremony. Gifts are typically given out by representatives of the Synagogue, youth groups, and sisterhoods at the conclusion of the Saturday Service. You can expect traditional Jewish gifts such as candlesticks, *Kiddush* cups, prayer books, *Tzedakah* boxes and a Bar or Bat Mitzvah certificate of completion.

If you would like to have a specific representative present a gift to your child, seek clergy approval in advance, and make sure they follow the guidelines. For example, the youth group gift can be presented to the Bar or Bat Mitzvah by their closest friends from Hebrew school class.

Make Hair Stylist, Pedicure, Manicure Appointments

Make beauty and grooming appointments for the week leading up to the Mitzvah. You don't want to wait too long and find that the schedule is full. The time spent taking care of yourself in the week leading up to the Bar or Bat Mitzvah will be cherished time to breathe and reflect in an otherwise very busy week.

1–2 Months Before the Event

☐ Mail Invitations (*6 Weeks Out*)

☐ Confirm RSVPs (*3 Weeks Out*)

☐ Confirm Date, Time, Schedule with All Vendors

☐ Guest List for Candle Lighting Ceremony (*optional*)

☐ Order Food for *Oneg Shabbat* and *Kiddush* luncheon

☐ Confirm and Complete Decorations

Mail Invitations

Invitations are typically mailed six weeks before the event. Once the invitations are mailed, give guests at least three weeks to reply.

Confirm RSVPs

After three weeks, follow up with guests who have not yet responded. It is okay to use modern technology to do this: email, call, or text and ask if they plan to attend. If you don't hear back immediately, it is a good idea to reach out using more than one method. Some people prefer to communicate by phone, while others prefer email or text. If you contact them using a couple of methods, it makes it easier to respond in their preferred manner.

When you reach out, ask first if they received the invitation, and if so, which entree they would like to order. If they did not receive the invitation, immediately follow up with a photo of the invite so that they have all the details. If they did receive it, asking about their meal preference will force your guest to make a decision and commit to your event, or politely decline.

Confirm Date, Time, Schedule with All Vendors

At a recent Bar Mitzvah that we attended, the DJ called the host 2 hours before the event started and mistakenly set up at a different location. To avoid this mishap, confirm and solid-ify schedules with all vendors that you have hired, including bands, DJ, photographer, videographer, florist, and any addi-tional entertainment providers.

Guest List for Candle Lighting Ceremony (*optional*)

If you are planning a candle lighting ceremony, create a list of honorees and write excerpts about each person. Again, see more on the candle lighting ceremony in Chapter 11.

Order Food for *Oneg Shabbat* and *Kiddush* Luncheon

Order food for the Friday night *Oneg Shabbat* and Saturday afternoon *Kiddush* luncheon through your synagogue office if you have not already made arrangements with an outside caterer. Remember temple or synagogue regulars will attend these meals, so give the office the number of guests you ex-pect, and they will combine those numbers with the regulars to get an expected headcount.

If you are hosting a lunch celebration at a restaurant for your Bar or Bat Mitzvah guests outside of the *Kiddush*, commu-nicate your plan with the office. That way they will know to order food for regulars only.

Synagogues have experience for how much food to order and what guests like to eat, so ask them for help. Some synagogues allow outside vendors to cater food for the luncheon, while others only cater in-house. If you hire an outside vendor, they will most likely need to adhere to Kosher standards and be approved by the synagogue ahead of time. Synagogues that allow outside caterers will have preapproved vendor lists.

Confirm and Complete Decorations

Make sure decorations are locked down for the celebration: centerpieces, balloons, guest book, sign-in board, *Havdalah* candles, etc. Confirm fresh flower pickup or delivery with the florist.

Gather everything in one place so that you have it ready to go on the day of the event. You may wish to have one storage area for the ceremony, where you include things such as the candy, *kippot,* and *tallitot,* and another for the celebration, where you include things like the centerpieces, party favors, candles, and so on.

1 Week Before the Event

- ☐ Finalize Day-of-Event Schedule

- ☐ Make Checklist of Items to Take to Ceremony and Celebration

- ☐ Send Final Headcount to Caterer

- ☐ Finalize Seating Arrangements

- ☐ Hair, Manicure, Pedicure Appointments

- ☐ Formal Photos (*optional*)

- ☐ Confirm Sunday Brunch Reservations (*if hosting brunch*)

- ☐ Arrange Transportation for Out-of-Town Guests (*optional*)

- ☐ Drop off Hotel Guest Gift Bags (*optional*)

Finalize Day-of-Event Schedule

Make sure you have a master list of everything that will happen on the day of the event, from what time you need to leave your house, to what time you'll arrive at the synagogue and the ceremony, who you need to meet with (e.g., clergy, caterers, DJ, event planner), when and what people will eat, dance and catering schedules, and so on.

Make sure you have phone numbers to contact any and all vendors in case of unexpected bumps in the road.

Make Checklist of Items to Take to Ceremony and Celebration

Make a checklist of all items you need to take to the synagogue and the reception and work out the logistics of how you will get the items to the correct location. Make sure you have everything prepared and ready to go.

Some items for the synagogue include: parent and teen speeches, *Tallitot*, *kippot* (yarmulkes), candy (for the candy throwing ritual mentioned in Chapter 8), and bags to collect gifts.

Some items for the reception include: gifts for guests, bags to collect presents that your Bar or Bat Mitzvah receives, slide projector and screen, guest book and pens, centerpieces, candelabra, and candles and lighters for the candle lighting ceremony. It's always a good idea to have a small emergency pack with things like safety pins, bobby pins, Band-Aids, stain remover, mint, etc.

If you aren't going home between the ceremony and the celebration, also remember a change of clothes and shoes, and any jewelry or accessories.

Send Final Headcount to Caterer

Confirm menu, final headcount, and entrée selections with the caterer. Be sure to read your contract to know the deadline on when to send your final headcount numbers. Some caterers or venues may require more than one week's notice.

Finalize Seating Arrangements

Print any last minute table seating cards and shuffle seating arrangements in case of cancellations or additions.

Hair, Manicure, Pedicure Appointments

Take care of yourself, and make sure you feel beautiful and ready to host an unforgettable Bar or Bat Mitzvah.

Formal Photos (*optional*)

It is common to take formal photos, including pictures on the *Bimah*, with the Rabbi and Cantor the week before the Bar or Bat Mitzvah. It makes for a great memory, but it is optional.

I didn't feel I had the time or energy to get all dolled up—we were still so busy running around to prepare for the big day. However, if you want to preserve the moment with formal photos, set up an appointment with the office, and make arrangements with your photographer. Keep in mind this will incur an additional cost. Ask a friend to take photos if you want to save money. If you do decide on formal photos with the clergy, try to schedule them for a date after your hair and nail appointments.

Instead of the photo shoot, I opted to set up a video camera in a room off to the side, with a clear view of the ceremony, before *Shabbat* began. I was able to ask a synagogue employee to turn the camera on before the morning service. That way, we were able to capture the event as it unfolded and avoid the extra trip to the synagogue.

Check with your temple guidelines regarding video equipment during the ceremony. We were allowed to set it up ahead of time, but could not hit record on the *Shabbat*. The office staff was more than happy to help us record the moment.

Confirm Sunday Brunch Reservations

If you are hosting a Sunday brunch, call the restaurant to confirm the reservation, making sure the restaurant has the right time and number of guests.

Arrange Transportation for Out-of-Town Guests (*optional*)

If you opted to provide guest transportation to and from the airport and the hotel, be sure to book transportation according to flight plans. In addition to taxis and hotel shuttles, you may consider ride-sharing services such as Uber or Lyft. Taking care of transportation details is a nice option if you want to do something extra for your out-of-town guests, but it is not necessary. If you are feeling short on time or budget, skip it.

Drop Off Hotel Guest Gift Bags (*optional*)

If you decided to provide gift bags for hotel guests, deliver gifts one to two days before they arrive. Drop them off at the front desk of the hotel. Be sure you have correct hotel reservation details for each guest, including reservation name and arrival and departure details, so that the gifts arrive in the right hands. You should have coordinated delivery details and fees with the hotel in advance. (*See three-month timetable details.*)

Chapter 5
Guest Protocol and Expectations

The surest way to host a Bar or Bat Mitzvah that guests will remember fondly is to set expectations right from the start.

Inform vendors exactly what is expected of them, including when and where you need their services, and ask them how you can help ensure a smooth event as the host.

Answer questions that non-Jewish guests may have about the ceremony and the celebration. This may be done preemptively, as guests may be shy to ask questions for wont of seeming naïve or ignorant.

Have open discussions with your young teen and with your synagogue about the spiritual and traditional elements that make the day meaningful.

Finally, as guests arrive, set the tone and make them feel welcome and comfortable, while encouraging them to connect and respect the sanctity of the event.

In this chapter, you will find the most common questions that non-Jews ask or wonder about the Bar or Bat Mitzvah, as well as tips to minimize cell phone use at the event, so that guests remember the conversation and connection long after the event is over, not a handheld screen.

Setting Expectations: Tips for Everyone

Below are a few things that everyone, from the hosts to the Bar or Bat Mitzvah to the vendors to the guests should know. You may want to speak with your Rabbi to find out how best to communicate the tips to everyone.

- In most synagogues, men are required to wear a *kippah/yarmulke* (head covering). Ask your synagogue to verify local policy.

- Prayer Books are sacred. They should be placed in the pocket under the seat in front of you, never on the floor.

- Do not smoke anywhere on the synagogue premises.

- Do not take photos or videos on the synagogue premises. You may be able to ask your synagogue or temple if you could set up a video recorder in a side or back room the day before the Mitzvah and have a staff member press play. This should not be done by the Bar or Bat Mitzvah family.

- Avoid chewing gum.

- Silence all cell phones and text messaging.

- Refrain from writing.

Guidelines For Non-Jews

It is rare that a Bar or Bat Mitzvah has only Jewish guests. If you are inviting non-Jews or anyone who has not been to a Bar or Bat Mitzvah in many years, you may want to include a website link in your invitation.

If you have time, you can make your own website with a guest FAQ, or you can direct guests to an existing page. Invite everyone to view the website, as you will want to communicate answers to questions that all of your guests will have.

The website should include details for all guests about your event and celebratory details. Don't forget to share information about when to be at the synagogue and where it is located, when and where to expect lunch and dinner, what will be on the menu, and any specifics about parking for the ceremony and celebration.

If your child plans to invite a friend whose parents will not attend, be sure that the parents know exactly when and where to drop off and pick up their child.

Also share more general information for non-Jewish friends, such as a Bar or Bat Mitzvah definition, dress code, and more about Jewish traditions.

The following questions are primarily reflective of what non-Jewish friends and family want to know. They were the questions we were asked when planning my daughter's Bat Mitzvah, as well as some of the questions people recommended we address while researching to prepare for this guide. You can feel free to phrase the answers in your own way or borrow from us. Please reference this planning guide if you share the information online!

How much should I spend on a gift?

In Jewish tradition, giving a cash gift in multiples of $18 is very common. The tradition behind this is that the number eighteen in Hebrew is *Chai,* which means "life" in English. Giving a gift in multiples of $18 is known as "giving Chai" or the "gift of Chai," which essentially translates to giving the gift of life.

Therefore, many people give gifts in multiples of $18 (such as $18, $36, $54, $72, etc.). This is true not only for B'nai Mitzvah, but for all Jewish celebrations. Giving in multiples of $18 is like giving a gift and a blessing at the same time. We heartily recommend this wonderful tradition.

We've found that non-Jewish friends love to learn about the tradition of *Chai* and appreciate the opportunity to participate.

If the guest prefers to consider a non-cash gift, the item should be age appropriate for a twelve- or thirteen-year-old.

As the parents of the Bar or Bat Mitzvah, you know your child's interests. No guest wants to show up with a series of Harry Potter books, only to find out the Bar or Bat Mitzvah would rather play video games than read a book. People want to know that they are giving a gift that the child will like and use. It's okay to share hobbies and interests to steer them in the right direction.

Be aware that guests will give gifts according to their budget, and how well and for how long they know the family. That is to be expected.

A guest who has known your child since they were a baby may want to put more thought into the gift, give something heartfelt and maybe more expensive.

A guest who has only known your family for a short time or has a tight budget may scale down on the amount of the gift. There are still many nice, thoughtful gifts that are affordable, and you can share ideas if they ask.

Jewish themed gifts like Jewish Star pendants are lovely and available online as well as in your local Jewish store. However, they may be too common. When I was a Bat Mitzvah, I received so many Jewish Star pendants that I didn't know what to do with them all. Now I give out Proof Eagle Coins from the U.S. Mint. The kids go wild over them because it is a unique gift they do not often see, and something they will likely keep forever.

You may also want to share with guests—generally through a grapevine of trusted advisors rather than directly outright, that a generous gift is customary, depending on the number of people invited from their family.

Keep this section on gift-giving in mind the next time you are invited to your next Bar or Bat Mitzvah, and be transparent in sharing your thoughts and experiences with non-Jews who feel unsure of what to give. The gift is an opportunity to thank the host and hostess for their generosity.

What should I wear?

The Bar or Bat Mitzvah dress code is typically not announced on the invitation, so you may find that several guests reach out with questions.

A good rule of thumb is that most of your guests will likely follow is: Always dress up if you don't know what to wear. Suits or slacks and a tie for the men are common. As it is a religious event, women generally wear something modest, like a dress or suit. It is best to keep any skirt below the knees and avoid exposing too much. This goes for the hosts as well as guests since you set the tone.

If the Bar Mitzvah is an Orthodox event, women will need to wear long sleeves and a long skirt, as showing too much skin is considered immodest.

What can I expect at the ceremony?

The Bar or Bat Mitzvah will read from the Torah during the Saturday morning service and chant several prayers for both the Friday and Saturday morning service. Most prayers will be in Hebrew. If guests desire to follow along, the books generally contain the English translation.

We've found that guests often say they gain valuable insights from the text, which gives more meaning to the event and helps them feel more connected to the service.

Let guests know that a two-and-a-half to three-hour service is typical. They should expect a long service and plan accordingly (unless they plan to arrive fashionably late).

The Saturday morning *Shabbat* service can start around 9:30 a.m. and last until about noon. Since much of it will be in Hebrew, it can feel like an especially long time to those unfamiliar with the language.

You may want to tell guests who are not able to attend the full service that the Bar or Bat Mitzvah typically reads the Torah portion around 10:30 a.m., so they should plan on arriving before then.

Feel free to let close friends and family know that your teen will feel especially reassured and supported if they are able to arrive on time and stay for the full service.

What can I expect at the reception?

The celebration following the service varies from family to family. Many families save for the Bar or Bat Mitzvah from them time their child was a baby and go all out, while other families have more restrained budgets and host modest, yet heartfelt celebrations.

There are often activities, games, dancing and plenty of good food and drinks. Naturally, the larger the budget, the more elaborate the food and entertainment may be, but no matter the budget, expect something to eat and activities to connect with other guests.

Some families keep Kosher and only offer Kosher selections.

Guests should know that a full lunch is typically offered after the ceremony, so they may want to save room for dinner knowing there will be quite a bit to eat throughout the day.

What else should I know?

Check the resources section in the rear of this book for a helpful FAQ link from *My Jewish Learning* (www.myjewishlearning.com) that you can share with guests, or use to inform conversations.

Now, let's move on to an issue that applies to all guests.

Create a Cell Phone Policy

One common complaint is that teens and adults spend time on their cell phones during the reception instead of paying attention to what's going on or interacting with one another. That's frustrating for the host and other guests.

As a host, you paid a lot of money and put a lot of time into the event, and the last thing you want is for guests to be distracted. There are ways to handle this, from setting expectations, to formulating an official policy, to making the celebration too fun to tune out.

The best way to handle it is to make your party so engaging that it doesn't become an issue. As you read through the chapter on the celebration, pay attention to the variety of entertainment, dancing, food, games and spiritual elements to keep things fresh and your guests entertained and engaged.

I was worried about cell phones too, and I shared my concerns with the band. Our bandleader promised he had ways to address cell phone usage if it came up. In the end, we didn't need to worry because everyone was engaged and having so much fun that they automatically shut off their phones.

I always think that cell phone use is a good gauge to measure whether your party is successful or not. A little bit of usage is normal—people enjoy taking pictures and may need to communicate with caretakers or address emergencies. But if people are using their cell phones most of the time, the celebration may not be catered enough to the guest experience. The best way to engage guests is to look at the entire day through their eyes, from the ceremony to the celebration, and plan and set expectations accordingly.

I recommend that you create a cell phone policy and make it known in advance.

These days, it is normal for Rabbis to announce that guests should silence all cell phones when the ceremony begins. Check with your Rabbi to see if they can mention the celebration at that time as well. It is not too much to ask to let your guests know ahead of time what your cell phone policy is.

This can be done in person, on your website if you create one, via email, or even on the invitation. If you hire a professional to design your invitation, ask how you can do this tastefully.

It is also common now to post a sign at the entrance to a celebration stating a no cell phone policy. Often it is worded in such a way that it invites guests to unplug and enjoy the evening. Perhaps you've seen such a sign at a recent wedding or milestone birthday celebration.

If you choose to announce the policy out loud when the celebration begins, keep your announcement lighthearted and clear. For example, "We welcome everyone and please kindly consider unplugging this evening."

Also, if you are against guests posting pictures on social media, let them know when you make the announcement about cell phones. I would advise against including such a request on the invitation itself, but you may be able to post it to your event website.

Game to Disarm Cell Phone Users

Pileup is an easy suggestion that simply asks everyone to pile all of their smartphones on top of each other in the middle of the dinner table and keep them there until the end of the event.

If you want to add a little fun and make it a game, up the ante with a stipulation that the first one to pick up their cell phone before pileup is over must buy drinks for everyone or pay them money. That way everyone else wins, and your guests will be happy to support the policy!

Chapter 6
Set a Budget

The first question that you should ask yourself when planning the events surrounding the Mitzvah is: How much do I want to spend?

It is also important to ask the question: How much should I realistically expect to spend? Bar and Bat Mitzvahs, as with any major life event, can be more costly than one might imagine. It's good to walk in with realistic expectations, while at the same time determining what your family can afford.

Create a budget based on your financial decision, and try to avoid going beyond it. It possible, do not touch college savings or emergency funds set aside for a rainy day.

We have outlined several celebration options below to work within your budget constraints, from low-end to high-end.

Low-End Budget Options

Kiddush **Luncheon**

The *Kiddush* luncheon is a lunch immediately following the Saturday morning service, generally lasting a maximum of two hours. It consists of food and schmoozing with guests and can be used as a simplified celebration. The *Kiddush* luncheon is usually a requirement for all Bar and Bat Mitzvahs, so it is an expense that you will incur.

If you are on a seriously tight budget, you can get away with just the luncheon as a celebration, and maybe include a Sunday brunch and Friday night dinner at your house.

This is the most inexpensive option you can choose. Keep in mind that connecting with guests is what is important during this special time, and know that temple regulars will be part of the celebration if you choose this option.

Restaurant Luncheon

As an alternative, if you are not observant, directly following the service, you can forgo the Kiddush luncheon, and have your guests drive directly to a local restaurant to celebrate the Bar or Bat Mitzvah child. Be aware that you will still need to pay for the *Kiddush* luncheon for regulars who attend Saturday morning services.

You can choose most any type of restaurant you like (Italian, Kosher Chinese, sushi, traditional Jewish deli, etc.) that has the space and will work with a large enough reservation to accommodate your guests.

Tip

Always try to keep the location of the restaurant or reception near the ceremony. If the drive is too far, it can be a deterrent for guests. If they sense that the travel experience is too complicated or too far, guests may opt out of the celebratory part of your Mitzvah. Make it easy for them to fully participate in the day's events.

Mid-Level Budget Options

Kids-Only Party

This is a party for friends of the Bar or Bat Mitzvah only and is not recommended. It can occur directly after the ceremony or on a Saturday night or on a Sunday. Sometimes people choose this option because they feel the Mitzvah event schedule focuses more on the adults, and they feel the child may want a "fun" party of their own at a place like the local science center, a maritime or aviation museum, a golf and arcade center, bowling arcade, waterpark, aquarium or yacht club.

This is not something that I would recommend. Such an event may save money compared to a traditional reception, but it should be considered more of an option for a birthday party rather than a religious rite of passage.

B'nai Mitzvot are reverent and religious in nature and tend to reflect spiritual elements such as holiness, while birthday parties are typically non-secular. While the Bar or Bat Mitzvah generally occurs near the child's actual birthday, it should be reserved as a special ceremony and celebration, with its own significance.

Also know that a kids-only party can make people feel left out, while the Bar or Bat Mitzvah celebration should be all about including the community. Excluding people from cele-brations based on age truly goes against Torah values.

Tip

I highly recommend that you avoid treating your child's Bar or Bat Mitzvah like a birthday party celebration. It is a growing trend, but I advise against it. This is a holy event, and it's important to make a distinction between birthdays and B'nai Mitzvot. Avoid common birthday activities such as video game trucks, trampolines, paintball, etc.

Afternoon Celebration

This option combines all of the traditional aspects of a recep-tion—cocktail hour, music, entertainment, food, drinks, but it is less formal than an evening party in both guest attire and event experience. Because it is in the day, there is a different feel to it.

One bonus is that since daytime isn't as busy for vendors, you may be able to negotiate some great deals.

Most temples and synagogues have a reception room that you may be able to reserve. By hosting the reception in the same place as the ceremony, you'll make it easy for guests to attend both.

High-End Budget Options

Evening Celebration

While similar to an afternoon party in content, the evening party starts between 6:00 and 7:00 p.m., and is generally more formal.

This celebration suits all denominations but has an additional bonus of catering to the religious who observe *Shabbat* restrictions. The protocol for *Shabbat* would be to wait until sundown before the reception begins. Be aware that this can be quite late in the summer months, especially in northern latitudes.

One common complaint that I have heard about evening receptions is that dinner wasn't served until after 9:00 p.m., so guests were hungry, and those who wanted to be home relatively early for bed had to wait a long time to leave. Make sure you think about your guests and serve food at an appropriate hour if you select an evening party. Appetizers will help with the hunger.

Nightclubs (Lounges)

Although not traditional by any means, this is a unique venue that can be very exciting for you child. They get a taste of a grown-up experience, seeing how a DJ or band work outside of traditional events, and looking at the fluorescent lights and lounge decor, and different food and drinks.

You can rent out the entire club or just a reception room in a club or lounge. Although this type of party may leave the teens with amazing memories, it can be loud and dark and may not be suited for older guests and younger kids. Remember, the Bar or Bat Mitzvah should feel inclusive for all generations.

Additional Meals

If you have out-of-town guests, it is a nice gesture to include them in Friday night and Sunday morning meals. You may also wish to include family and close friends, such as those honored in the candle ceremony discussed in Chapter 11, and those helping with readings and ceremonial honors, as discussed in Chapter 8.

Friday Night *Shabbat* Dinner

The Friday night *Shabbat* dinner provides an intimate setting to start the Mitzvah weekend and is a nice touch to honor out-of-town guests, family, and close friends. This is separate from the *Oneg Shabbat* discussed in Chapter 8.

You may host the *Shabbat* dinner at a restaurant or in your home. Hosting at a restaurant saves time and effort of having guests over, while hosting at home saves money. This dinner is highly recommended but should be considered optional. If you choose to host it, don't worry about inviting all of the Bar or Bat Mitzvah guests. This is a more intimate experience designed for those who traveled from out of town, and family and friends who are closest to the family.

Sunday Brunch

If you're expecting several out-of-town guests who will be staying at a hotel, it's nice to offer brunch at a local restaurant or private room. This allows you an additional opportunity to see friends and family who have traveled from afar to celebrate the special day with you and your family. Since the large event is over and done with, you'll feel more relaxed and able to offer your full time and attention.

If you want to scale down on costs, invite guests to stop by your home and host an informal get-together. You can make a simple spread with fruit, pastries, deli sandwiches, and hot beverages that will be appreciated by all, or you can offer more variety. Remember to pick up brunch food the week or day before the Bar or Bat Mitzvah or arrange to have it delivered, as you'll be too tired from the weekend festivities to go shopping on Sunday morning.

Synagogue and Mitzvah Fees

When you're budgeting, be sure to include the one-time Mitzvah service fee charged for ceremony preparation. All membership dues should be kept up to date, as an outstanding balance could potentially postpone your child's celebration.

Fees vary between synagogues, but costs that you may be expected to pay (if not build into the membership fee) include:

- Past Due and Annual Membership Fees

- Bar or Bat Mitzvah Tutors

- Materials, Books and Folders

- Friday night service *Oneg Shabbat*

- Use of the Sanctuary and Temple Personnel on Saturday

- Saturday Morning *Kiddush* Luncheon

Additional Expenses

There are several additional expenses to consider. The more elaborate your *simcha*, the more expensive each line item will be.

Many of the expenses below can be considered optional, or you can get creative and do some of it yourself to save money. For example, if you have a large garden, you may consider using your own cut flowers rather than going through a florist.

- Decorations and Flowers

- Theme-Related Décor

- Centerpieces

- Entertainers

- Invitations and RSVP Cards, Thank You Cards and Save the Date Cards (Plus Envelopes and Postage for All of These)

- Photographer and Videographer

- Catering: Food, Drinks, Appetizers

- Clothing, Shoes and Accessories

- Personal Grooming Appointments for Hair and Nails

- Hotel and Venue

- Music, Including Bands and/or DJs

- Hotel Room Blocks

- Gifts for Guests or Celebration Games

- Parking

Chapter 7
Communications:
Invitations and Cards

Communication is important, and your guests will appreciate a formal invitation and handwritten thank you note. Check the timeline for a reminder of when to send out save the dates and invitations.

Let's begin with initial communication, and then move through all remaining communication in order up through the thank you cards.

Save The Date Cards

As we've already established, planning for the Bar or Bat Mitzvah begins far in advance—up to two years out, and takes time and money. Protect your investment, and give guests a heads up about the date, time and place of your Mitzvah at least a year in advance.

The ultimate objective of save the date cards is to get your guests to show up for the monumental event. Invitations go out about six weeks prior to the event, but people's calendars tend to book up much earlier than that. Advance notice will ensure your guests can make the Bar or Bat Mitzvah a priority. Save the dates are especially important to out-of-town guests who need to arrange hotel and flight reservations.

Invitations

We used a professional invitation consultant because she is a dear friend and we appreciated her expertise.

However, you can save a lot of money by doing it yourself. Check out Shutterfly or similar invitation websites to print the invitations at a fraction of the cost. Online sites have several styles already designed, so you can plug in the information specific to your Bar or Bat Mitzvah and create something that looks great.

The selection and variety of invitations can be overwhelming. I find that keeping it simple saves you from getting bogged down by the multitude of options that exist. To make things even easier, you can upload guests' addresses. The company will then mail the invitations directly to guests, saving you time. A word of caution though: I have used this service for birthday parties and found that some of my guests did not receive their invitation. You will need a process to validate and ensure that invitations were mailed to all of our guests.

Since we went with an invitation specialist and since our guest list was not complete when we ordered the invitations, we printed out our own address labels.

Invitations should be sent six weeks prior to the event, but can take some time to print. You'll want to plan and design them closer to three months ahead of the event, just in case you run into any issues.

Don't be tempted to save money with an electronic invitation like Evite. The invitation sets the tone for the Mitzvah, and a certain level of formality is appropriate. The invitation should generate excitement, something that hard copy invitations convey better than their electronic counterparts.

If you selected a theme for the Bar or Bat Mitzvah, or if you'd like to tie in what the guests can expect for decorations, it's a nice touch to include a little nod to the celebration itself on or in the invitation. We added peacock feathers to our invitations, which complemented our centerpieces and gave guests a peak into the decorations to come.

The advantage to using a professional when selecting invitations is that they have direct connections with printers and designers, so if something goes wrong, they can help fix it.

It happened to us. When we received the invitations, we found that the feathers were slightly damaged. Our invitation consultant was able to return them at no charge to us, and we were sent a new batch of invitations.

This is also one reason you should order the invitations some time in advance of sending them out. Start planning invitations up to six months in advance, as it takes time to decide a favorite style, then place the order about three months prior to the Bar or Bat Mitzvah. That way you'll have just over a month to receive your order and send it back if there are any issues.

Invitations set the stage and generate excitement for your guests. I was so enthralled with the Bat Mitzvah invitations I received when I was a child that I still have them to this day.

Make yours special and unique for your guests.

RSVP Cards

It is highly encouraged to include a card in the invitation so guests can RSVP. Include space to fill out their name, how many people will be attending, and their meal preference.

At the bottom, include the RSVP "respond by" date, which should be three weeks prior to the Bar or Bat Mitzvah.

Tip

You may run into situations where only the adults or children are invited from certain families. If you don't intend to invite everyone from the family, you can add on the RSVP card exact names or the number of people invited.

If you include an RSVP card, you must include a postage paid, pre-addressed return envelope so that guests can easily fill out the card and drop it in the mail.

There is a growing trend to swap out the RSVP card and replace it with an email address or RSVP website, encouraging a digital reply. While it is an option, and may seem tempting in today's instant online world, I believe that it is not the preferred option. Remember, the goal is to make it as simple as possible to RSVP and attend your child's Bar or Bat Mitzvah. Personally, I feel an email request might take more effort or be more easily forgotten than dropping a pre-paid envelope in the mail, but you know your guests best. Just remember, any delay in reply leaves headcounts up in the air.

My best recommendation is to opt for an RSVP card—unless you are on a tight budget and looking for tips to save money where you can, or you're partial to technology.

Electronic RSVPs

If you choose to forgo the printed RSVP card, you might consider using a website to manage and track replies.

Online RSVP websites allow you to choose a unique URL, customize your design, add menu selections, monitor RSVP counts, and add custom questions for your guests. You can embed the link or the form on your event website, or you can print the link on your hard copy invitations.

It also allows you to easily see guests who haven't replied.

I advise you to tread lightly when it comes to electronic RSVPs as I have attended Bar and Bat Mitzvahs where website glitches caused big problems for the guests and the hosts alike. Common complaints were that guests were not able to access the website, there were issues with the site configuration, and RSVP responses were lost and not tracked.

Personalized Mitzvah Websites

If you want a platform that provides a more comprehensive look and feel for what to expect at your Bar or Bat Mitzvah, consider building a website to connect with your guests.

These days, there are plenty of ways to build a simple site in a matter of a few hours.

You can use a website to display before and after event photos, add important information about the full weekend event schedule, including Friday evening services, dinner arrangements, maps and directions to the synagogue and reception, transportation options, hotels in the area and blocks of rooms that you have reserved (if applicable), as well as Sunday Brunch information.

RSVP forms can be customized and a spreadsheet file (CSV) can be downloaded for sorting and organizing. One advantage to using a website is that you can simplify your invite. You'll no longer need to include a special card with information such as maps, directions and hotel information.

To find companies that provide such websites, you can search in Google by typing in the keywords "Bar Mitzvah website."

MyEvent is one company for you to consider when creating your personalized website. Find it at mitzvahs.myevent.com. The site is free and simple to use.

Table Seating Cards

Make your own table seating cards for ultimate flexibility and to adhere to a budget-friendly option.

We printed our own table seating assignments at home and they turned out beautifully. By going this route, you will be able to handle last-minute changes in seating (and I guarantee there will be a few!) and fix any issues with spelling or name changes as they come up.

Some people use a professional printer, which is fine. However, that means you will need to lock down the guest list and seating assignments far in advance, and your options to change things will be limited.

We used Avery place cards. They were very easy to use and cost less than $25. Avery has downloadable templates that work with your home printer, and it is as simple as filling out the names and table numbers. Go to avery.com/templates.

Thank You Cards

Thank you cards are wonderful because they teach your child the art of being gracious. In today's instant online climate, a handwritten thank you may feel like an outdated tradition, but it's not. Good manners and a kind word in print transcend time and should be reinforced.

Even though it can be a time-consuming task, it is important to acknowledge guests for the gift that they bestowed upon your child.

Do not write the thank you cards for your child. This is a task that should be done by them since it teaches and encourages self-discipline. The Bar or Bat Mitzvah is a coming of age ceremony, and this is a responsibility that your child can take on.

But remember, it doesn't have to be done all at once.

If your child feels overwhelmed, break the task into smaller pieces and encourage your child write three or four per day.

As your child is opening gifts, be sure to record the name of the person and the associated gift so that it is easy to refer to the list and make sure that a personalized thank you card was sent to everyone who attended, and everyone who sent a gift but could not make the event.

The thank you card can be designed and ordered along with your invitations if you want a single coordinated theme for both, or you can buy a pack of thank you cards online or at any local stationery or greeting card store.

Each thank you card should have the following components:

- guest's name,

- what the gift was,

- how much you liked the gift,

- what you intend to do with the gift (*optional*), and

- acknowledgement for sharing in your *simcha* (celebration).

Look at the sample note below for an idea of what the thank you card should say. Be sure to replace the words in parentheses and italics with your own note.

Sample Thank You Card

Dear (*Guest Name*),

Thank you so much for attending my (*Bar or Bat*) Mitzvah and celebrating with me. I really appreciate (*your generous gift*). It was very thoughtful and I plan to (*use the money to purchase a new computer*). It meant the world to me that you were there and I feel blessed that you could join me.

Many Hugs,

(*Your Name*)

Chapter 8
The Ceremony

The ceremony guide is for those who want a deeper understanding of rituals and an overview of what to expect. What we describe here a generalized version of what goes on at a "typical" Bar or Bat Mitzvah.

I use the word "typical" lightly. There is truly no standard or uniform approach to the Mitzvah. Every synagogue has its own procedures and practices that may differ significantly from what is described here. You must consult with your synagogue or temple for the specifics of your service.

This chapter should familiarize you with aspects of the ceremony that may be discussed at the ceremony planning sessions and should be used as a general guide. However, you may wish to take notes in the margins, detailing similarities and differences between what you read here, and local practices.

A Bar or Bat Mitzvah usually consists of two services: one Friday night, and one Saturday morning. The Friday night service is the shorter of the two. Saturday morning includes Torah readings and other rituals such as the Bar or Bat Mitzvah speech and parent speeches, discussed in this chapter.

Prepare Guests and Set Expectations

In addition to guest protocol set forth in Chapter 5, it is imperative to properly prepare guests unfamiliar with the Bar or Bat Mitzvah:

1. Inform guests that a large portion of the service will be in Hebrew. English translations are provided, but it can be challenging to follow along with the readings.

2. Let guests know that the Torah portion of the service can be quite lengthy. A traditional full Torah reading in an Orthodox synagogue—and some Conservative synagogues as well—can easily last 45–60 minutes. If the congregation follows the triennial tradition (splitting the Torah selection into three-year reading cycles) as some Conservative and most Reform synagogues do, it may take significantly less time.

Torah Readings and *Aliyot*

The core of the Bar or Bat Mitzvah ceremony is the Torah reading. The Torah is a collection of the first five books of the Hebrew Bible: Genesis, Exodus, Leviticus, Numbers, and Deuteronomy.

Every *Shabbat* (Saturday morning) in synagogue, a Torah reader chants a section from one of the five books. It is always done in Hebrew, in front of the entire congregation. This section is known as the weekly *Parsha* (Torah portion).

As noted above, there are two different traditions for which sections of the *Parsha* are chanted.

In Orthodox and some Conservative synagogues, the entire *Parsha* is chanted. Some Conservative and most Reform congregations read the *Parsha* on what's known as a triennial cycle. Approximately one-third of the "normal" *Parsha* is read so that it takes a total of three years for the full reading to be completed.

For more information about both traditions, and how the weekly Torah is chosen, see websites listed in the resources section at the back of this book.

The *Parsha* is further divided into seven separate readings, each known as an *Aliyah* (literally "going up" to [read] the Torah) and one additional reading after the *Kaddish* prayer called the *Maftir*.

Since there are different traditions of dividing the Torah reading into *Aliyot* (plural of *Aliyah*), you must follow your synagogue's guidance and policy. Each *Aliyah* is accompanied by two blessings, one said before and the other after the Torah reading.

The *Maftir* (last) *Aliyah* is chanted and read by the Bar or Bat Mitzvah.

The other *Aliyot* are usually given as honors to close family and friends. As the host, be sure to give honorees ample notice so they can practice and prepare. In the timeline, we recommend doing this no later than three months prior to the event.

We have included printed guides in Hebrew, transliterated into Roman characters, and translated into English below to assist readers. Links to YouTube videos that may help readers with pronunciation can be found in the resources section at the back of this book.

Following is the text of the blessings read before and after the Torah reading, in Hebrew and English. The translations come from Wikipedia.

Synagogues usually have printouts available for guests, but you are welcome to make copies or email the next couple of pages to your honored readers in advance.

Blessing Before Reading the Torah

In a confident voice, the *Oleh* (person saying the blessing) says:

בָּרְכוּ אֶת יְיָ הַמְבֹרָךְ

Oleh (transliteration): *Barchoo et-Adonai hamvorah.*

Translation: "You will bless The Lord who is to be blessed."

The congregation responds with the traditional blessing:

בָּרוּךְ יְיָ הַמְבֹרָךְ לְעוֹלָם וָעֶד

Congregation (transliteration):
Baruch Adonai hamvorah l'olam va'ed.

Translation: "Bless The Lord who is to be blessed forever and eternally."

The *Oleh* repeats the blessing just uttered by the congregation, then adds:

בָּרוּךְ אַתָּה יְיָ אֱלֹהֵינוּ מֶלֶךְ הָעוֹלָם, אֲשֶׁר
בָּחַר בָּנוּ מִכָּל הָעַמִּים, וְנָתַן לָנוּ אֶת תּוֹרָתוֹ. בָּרוּךְ אַתָּה יְיָ,
נוֹתֵן הַתּוֹרָה.

Oleh (transliteration): *Baruch atah Adonai, Eloheynu melech ha'olam.*

Asher bahar-banu mikal-ha'amim ve'notan-lanu es-torato.

Baruch atah Adonai, notayn ha-torah.

Translation: "Blessed are You, O Lord our G-d, king of all existence, Who chose us from among all nations and who gave us your Torah. Blessed are You, O Lord, who gives the Torah."

Congregation: Amen.

Reading the Torah

The first *Aliyah* of the *Parsha* (Torah reading) follows. If a more skilled person is doing the recitation, the *Oleh* will follow along with the reading (using the scroll or a printed book) in a subdued voice, as will the members of the congregation.

Blessing after Reading the Torah

When the *Aliyah* is finished, the *Oleh* offers a concluding benediction:

בָּרוּךְ אַתָּה יְיָ אֱלֹהֵינוּ מֶלֶךְ הָעוֹלָם, אֲשֶׁר נָתַן לָנוּ תּוֹרַת אֱמֶת,
וְחַיֵּי עוֹלָם נָטַע בְּתוֹכֵנוּ. בָּרוּךְ אַתָּה יְיָ
נוֹתֵן הַתּוֹרָה.

Oleh (transliteration):
Baruch atah Adonai, Eloheynu melech ha'olam.
Asher notan-lanu Torat emes.
Ve'hayay olam nota betohaynu.
Baruch atah Adonai, notayn ha-torah.

Translation: "Blessed are You, O Lord our G-d, king of all existence, Who has given us the Torah of the truth, and life everlasting within us. Blessed are You, O Lord, who gives the Torah."

Congregation: Amen.

Be sure to check the resources section at the back of this book for the link to a good YouTube video to help your honorees practice.

Remember, the blessings will be read before and after each *Aliyah*.

Torah Honors: *Hagbah* and *G'lilah*

After the *Maftir* (final *Aliyah*) is read by the Bar or Bat Mitzvah, the Torah is lifted (*Hagbah*) and wrapped (*G'lilah*). These are two additional honors to give to close friends or family.

Once the reading of the Torah has concluded, but before the *Haftarah* is chanted, the Torah is raised and wrapped in preparation to be returned to the ark. As the Torah is raised, congregations chant, "This is the Torah that Moses set before the people Israel; the Torah, given by G-d, through Moses." After the Torah is wrapped but before it is put away, the *Maftir* recites the blessings before and after the *Haftarah* reading.

Hagbah

Lifting the Torah can be strenuous, so the task should only be given to someone who is physically fit. It is preferable to choose someone who has done it before.

Accidentally dropping the Torah during *Hagbah* would be a horrifying mistake for any a Bar or Bat Mitzvah. Do not underestimate how heavy and unwieldy a Torah is.

I attended one Bar Mitzvah where I watched as an older man lift the Torah above his head, and then beyond. The Torah swayed backward and was heading toward the floor when the Rabbi intervened and caught it midair.

Thankfully the clergy had prior experience in the art of catching a Torah.

G'lilah

G'lilah is an honor to bestow upon a Jewish adult, and it means dressing, or wrapping, the Torah.

Once the readings are complete, before returning the Torah to the Ark, it is wrapped and covered. You may wish to watch videos on YouTube for examples of how it's done, but rely on the clergy at your synagogue to give instructions on local customs. It is a beautiful tradition.

Haftarah Reading

After the Torah is wrapped, the Bar or Bat Mitzvah reads the *Haftarah*, which is a reading from a book of Prophets such as Isaiah or Jeremiah.

Sects of Judaism follow their own traditions of what to read, so there are distinct differences between *Haftarah* options amongst Ashkenazi (East European) and Sephardic (Spanish, Middle Eastern) Jews so check with your synagogue to learn which traditions are followed locally.

When the Bar or Bat Mitzvah concludes the final blessing, after reading the *Haftarah*, the highlight of the entire ceremony is at hand: the candy throwing! This is guaranteed to bring smiles to your guests' faces.

Candy Throwing Ritual

Throwing candy is based on the idea of "showering" the Bar or Bat Mitzvah with sweetness.

It is one of the most fun and interesting rituals at the ceremony and very special for guests and the Bar or Bat Mitzvah alike.

It is worth noting that the wrong candy (hard) in the wrong hands (children who have been forced to sit quietly for at least 1½ hours)—or even in the hands of adults who want to "nail" the Bar or Bat Mitzvah—can injure the Mitzvah teen as well as anyone in the line of fire.

Therefore we recommend using soft candies such as Starburst fruit chews. You can also check with your Rabbi for Kosher alternatives if you prefer not to use Starburst. Any candy that enters the sanctuary for use in a Jewish ritual must be Kosher.

Tip

Hide small bags of candy under the seats in the pocket for the Torah and prayer books! When you are preparing the bags, remember to provide enough for your guests, in addition to regulars who attend Saturday service.

To prevent noisy shuffling and awkwardly passing candy baskets down the rows of congregants that distract from the service, we came up with an innovative idea of hiding the candy in the seat pocket in front of each guest.

A few minutes before the candy throwing ritual, the Rabbi announced that there was candy and said where it was hidden.

The Rabbi loved our idea so much that he decided to use it in all future Bar and Bat Mitzvah ceremonies at our synagogue so that became our legacy.

Depending on your synagogue's timeline, parent and Bar or Bat Mitzvah speeches often follow the candy throwing ritual.

The Bar or Bat Mitzvah Speech

Synagogues usually publish guidelines to help the Bar or Bat Mitzvah write a speech. Guidelines may include requirements about the length of the speech (by time or word count), and suggestions to welcome and thank the key people who supported and helped the Bar or Bat Mitzvah achieve his or her goals. Key people usually include Rabbis, Cantors, teachers, parents and siblings.

The speech should include lessons learned throughout the Mitzvah process, in addition to reflections from the Torah and the *Haftarah* readings, and detailed information how the *Tikkun Olam* project was implemented. If you skipped the section on *Tikkun Olam*, be sure to read about the Mitzvah projects in Chapter 2.

Picture Courtesy: https://commons.wikimedia.org/wiki/

The speech can make or break the Bar or Bat Mitzvah, so help your teen commit the time to getting it right, and encourage them to practice so they are comfortable in front of an audience.

Additional Bar or Bat Mitzvah Speech Tips

- Offer gratitude and acknowledge everyone involved, whether present at the ceremony or not, including relatives who have recently passed.

- Remember to thank all of your family and give special thanks to out-of-town guests.

- Choose and research a passage, story or verse in your portion to focus upon and write why it is meaningful to you and how it applies to modern day life.

- Research Rabbinical authorities to see what they have to say about your Torah portion. Refer to the list of commentary websites on the weekly *Parsha* in the resources section at the end of this book for more information.

- Keep it short: five to seven minutes

- Humor is allowed, but don't intentionally embarrass anyone—especially siblings.

- Practice, practice, practice! You don't want to read your speech for the very first time in front of a huge group of people. Read it to your family or in front of a mirror. You can even ask someone to videotape you practicing, to see how you present.

- Remember to look up during your speech. Pause when you thank guests by name, and offer a smile if you can see them. And speak slowly so that everyone can hear and understand.

Sample Bat Mitzvah Speech

First, thank you all for being here to celebrate this special day with me. I would especially like to thank my mother and father who have been so supportive of me for the last thirteen years.

Also, a big thank you to my uncles, aunts, grandparents, brothers and sisters who have always been there for me, as well as my cousins who have traveled far to celebrate with me. For all of my friends that have been so kind to me over the years, I am beyond excited that you came to share in this moment. Lastly, I would like to thank the Cantor and Rabbi and my teachers for helping in the Bat Mitzvah preparation and for providing me with inspiration.

My Torah portion is called Vayera, and it is from the book Genesis, which is known in Hebrew as Bereshit. One particular part that stood out to me is when Abraham was sitting under a tree outside of his tent and in the distance he noticed three strangers. He rushed to greet them and made sure that they were comfortable and satisfied by providing them with food and shelter.

We are taught by this story that Abraham and Sarah were models for outstanding hospitality and knowing how to make people feel welcome. At my house, hospitality has been an important way of my life ever since I was born. My family strives to create a welcoming environment by making guests feel as comfortable as possible. We have large Thanksgiving Day dinners as well as many parties, and we always greet our guests and make them feel welcome by providing them with excellent cuisine. My parents work very hard when they entertain. My father is an excellent cook and my mother spends countless hours cleaning for their parties. Now that I am a Bat Mitzvah, I know this will change and I will have to start helping too!

As I stand before you and G-d on this day of my Bat Mitzvah, I think that hospitability is the key to a better understanding of people's different beliefs. If people could share a meal together, break bread, and talk over and communicate their differences, the world would be a better place.

For my Tikkun Olam project, I plan on donating a portion of my Bat Mitzvah money that I receive to help animals in need. There are animals all across the world that need help! I am especially concerned about captive animals like tigers that are stuck in cages their entire life, mother pigs that spend their entire life in a crate too small for them to turn around, and bears who are held captive and go blind because they are forced to fight dogs. I worry about baby elephants that are tracked down and taken from the wild by poachers. They suffer physical and psychological abuse until their wild spirit is broken, just so they can perform unnatural acts like giving rides to tourists. These animals are isolated, starved, beaten and chained up in small enclosures.

A portion of the money that I receive in gifts, I plan on sending to the World Animal Protection agency (www.worldanimalprotection.us.org). It will be used to help these poor animals and to provide sanctuaries *for them. They will receive food and water and be taken care of. They will be given a chance at a new life where they will be protected from the people who abuse them.*

Thanks again for coming and Shabbat Shalom.

The Parent Speeches

Parents will also have an opportunity to share personal blessings if desired. Usually these speeches are shorter, lasting around one to two minutes.

The speech should cover hopes and dreams for your child's future and positive reinforcement of virtues regarding their character.

Additional Parent Speech Tips:

- Focus on your child's strengths, particularly his or her character. Try to avoid speaking about your child's skill sets related to extracurricular activities.

- Make sure you emphasize how proud you are of them.

- Use humor wisely. Adding a touch of humor never hurts, but there is a fine line between sharing something "cute" and saying something your child will be truly embarrassed about. Please do not cause your child any public embarrassment or humiliation in the name of a humorous speech.

- Share your speech with the Rabbi in advance to validate its content and receive feedback and constructive criticism.

There are many professional speechwriters who can help if you are stuck, or if you feel insecure about your writing.

I recommend Ken Calof, who wrote the following speech for his daughter's Bat Mitzvah. It contains many key elements of good speechwriting. I've included Ken's email address in the resources section of this book.

Sample Parent Bat Mitzvah Speech

Ashley, There is a song by Joni Mitchell called "Big Yellow Taxi," and in it she sings, "Don't it always seem to go, that you don't know what you've got 'til it's gone?" Well we don't have to wait until your gone—whether it's off to college in another city, or to another place for a job, or married with a family of your own—to know what we've got. We have a beautiful, smart, funny young lady who can achieve whatever she puts her mind to. A woman who has the drive and determination that have continued over the years and have served you well, and made you a source of pride and inspiration for your mother, brother, sister and me. We have never been prouder of you than we are today seeing you up on the Bimah, making this covenant, this promise, with G-d and the Jewish people.

In a childhood book you and I used to read, the great philosopher and deep thinker Christopher Robin once said to his friend Winnie-the-Pooh, "Pooh, you are braver than you believe, stronger than you seem and smarter than you think."

Let's break that down as it applies to you…

Braver than you believe. *No matter what you have done in life, whether it was your first trip to overnight camp, leaving dance to try new things, or taking on the awesome task of preparing for today, you have bravely learned to meet challenges head-on and not only accomplished them but smashed through them. I promise that if you continue to meet life's challenges head-on like you have so far, you will make achieving your goals in life look easy.*

Stronger than you seem. *Bat Mitzvah, women in this family are deceptively strong and you are no exception. When you decide to do something in life, you don't just do it, you engulf it. Last year when you chose to leave dance, you didn't just quit and go home, you thought about what* *you wanted to do to enrich your life and have that transition make you stronger. You did just that, you embraced your Jewish culture and took in everything our Synagogue has to offer. You made lifelong friendships here and at school and you decided to learn to ice skate which you have continued to excel at. You have prepared yourself to stand strong and tall in the world, and we are confident that you will continue to accomplish anything and everything you set your mind to.*

Smarter than you think. *Bat Mitzvah, you are smart enough to do anything you choose. I sometimes think it's other people who may under-estimate your brilliance. Many people here don't know that you skipped a grade in school, and while that served you well in elementary school, your mother and I had some concerns about your transition to middle school. I remember when you started middle school, you told mom and me that you wanted to make the honor roll all three years. I just wanted you to get through it. I am proud to say, that so far you have kept your word of staying on the honor roll.*

Another story that comes to mind was when you started on this journey. We came to this Synagogue late in the game for you and I knew you had a huge task ahead of you to have a Bat Mitzvah. We sat in the Rabbi's office and talked about the challenges ahead of you and he told you that your Bat Mitzvah was about you and you could do as little or as much as you wanted and it would all work out. Without missing a beat, you said, "Rabbi, I like a challenge. Give me everything." I am not sure what he was thinking but I was proud that you wanted to take this on full force.

—Ken Calof

Friday Night *Oneg Shabbat* and Saturday *Kiddush* Luncheon

Food for the Friday night *Oneg Shabbat* and Saturday *Kiddush* luncheon needs to be prearranged with your synagogue and paid for in advance. See the timeline for more information about when to make arrangements.

Food for the *Kiddush* and *Oneg Shabbat* is mandatory in most synagogues. Be aware that it can cost a few thousand dollars so be prepared when setting your budget.

Most synagogues have menus with various price points. Rely on their guidance to know which dishes are popular and how much food to order. Assuming your guests will join in the *Kiddush* luncheon, they will need accurate headcounts to account for both visitors and regulars.

If you are hosting a luncheon for Bar or Bat Mitzvah guests in lieu of an evening celebration, be sure to let the synagogue know. If guests will not attend the *Kiddush* luncheon, you will only be asked to order food for the regulars.

If the *Kiddush* luncheon will take the place of an outside celebration, work with your synagogue to coordinate a schedule and any entertainment or decorations you wish to bring in. Be aware that congregants who regularly attend Saturday morning *Shabbat* services will be included in Bar or Bat Mitzvah celebrations unless you devote separate rooms: one for the regulars and another for guests. This is not a recommended practice since it does not reinforce inclusionary values.

If your synagogue allows outside caterers, ask about food policies and requirements, and then look into cost differences.

Friday Night *Oneg Shabbat* Selections

Friday night *Oneg Shabbat* options are relatively simple. They might include salads and an assortment of desserts.

Make sure you have enough food for the regulars as well as Bar or Bat Mitzvah guests attending Friday evening services and be as generous as possible within your budget when arranging this.

Saturday *Kiddush* Luncheon Selections

The following dishes are popular for the Saturday *Kiddush* luncheon:

- Fruit Platters
- Grilled Vegetables
- Tuna Salad
- Egg Salad
- Assorted Green Salads
- Kugel
- Pasta

- Quiche

- Wraps

- Challah

- Lox and Bagels

- Assorted Desserts

- Coffee and Tea

- Juice

- Wine

Decorations: Sanctuary and Luncheon

Synagogues strongly suggest providing some kind of decorative arrangement for the *Bimah* during the ceremony. It is an optional expense that is nice to have, but if you have exceeded your budget or you are saving all of your money for the celebration, you can consider opting out.

Tip

You might feel uncomfortable not decorating the Bimah since it seems as though everyone else does it, but please remember that it is optional unless your synagogue policy states that it is mandatory.

For my daughter's Bat Mitzvah, we opted out of decorations for the luncheon tables and sanctuary. This expense can cost thousands of dollars depending on how extravagant you are. Feel free to discriminate and make decisions based on your budget and time. Since the luncheon typically lasts at the most two hours, and the celebration is considerably longer, it might be a better value to save your Mitzvah dollars for the reception.

If you opt for the low-end budget option to host the celebration during the *Kiddush* luncheon, please do consider some decorations.

If you do decide to buy decorations for the sanctuary and luncheon, flowers have been popular historically speaking, but today's trend is to move toward *Tzedakah* arrangements. *Tzedakah* means to perform charitable acts and is a large part of Jewish faith. For example, your Bar or Bat Mitzvah child might want to make an arrangement of books, toys, balloons, stuffed animals or sports equipment, then distribute them to local shelters where kids may not have their own equipment and toys. Children who feel strongly about the issue of hunger might want to make a basket of nonperishable food items.

After the ceremony, *Tzedakah* baskets and floral arrangements can be broken apart and distributed to a local hospital, shelter, or nursing home. There are hundreds of organizations to donate to. Mazon: A Jewish Response To Hunger is a national nonprofit organization that allocates donations from the Jewish community to prevent and alleviate hunger among people of all faiths and backgrounds. For more information, visit their website at www.mazon.org.

Be sure to check with your synagogue office on height requirements for *Tzedakah* baskets and arrangements so as not to interfere congregants' visibility during the ceremony.

Chapter 9
Focus on the Guest Experience

Before we get into the specific elements of the Bar or Bat Mitzvah celebration, I wanted to include a section on making sure that guests of all ages, from young children through the elderly, will feel warmly welcomed and included.

I was asking some friends about Bar and Bat Mitzvahs they had recently attended.

"How was it?" I would ask.

"Completely disorganized!" they would reply.

Here was some of their feedback:

- "We didn't know which room to enter first."

- "Dinner was served an hour late."

- "The teens were all on their cell phones, including the Bat Mitzvah girl."

- "The dance floor was too small and people were tripping over each other during the *hora*."

- "I got trapped in the *hora* and couldn't get out."

- "There was no bread and butter on the tables."

- "There were no knives to cut food."

- "They provided plastic cups instead of real glass."

- "They served instant coffee instead of fresh-brewed."

- "There was no system for calling people to the buffet, so guests had to stand in long lines waiting for their food."

- "It was difficult to get ahold of a server. We could not get water for the table. The server did eventually bring one pitcher of water, which was barely enough for all of the people at our table."

- "There were no tables to eat appetizers so we had to hold our food and drink while standing."

- "We left before dessert due to loud music. It hurt our ears and we were concerned about hearing damage."

- "I wasn't able to sit at the same table with the people I knew."

- "My child sat with the adults instead of her friends."

- "The servers were bumping into the guests when refilling the trays of food at the buffet."

- "We were stuck on a train for four hours and we couldn't get off!"

Some of these issues could be addressed by setting expectations ahead of time, as we discussed in Chapter 5, but others are only avoided through careful planning and good communication with vendors.

Get Organized

It should go without saying that you don't want to leave your guests with a bad impression like those shared above. In each case, an event that should have been memorable for all the right reasons ended up memorable only as a disaster. If guests leave the celebration with a bad taste in their mouth, it could impact how they will view future B'nai Mitzvot, and they may even hesitate to accept another invitation in the future. Especially non-Jewish guests.

So please, do your research and plan wisely to make sure that these things don't happen to you. Stay as organized as possible.

I find it helps to create a road map laying out your list of reception activities and a schedule from your guest's perspective. Include everything on it, from when they will eat and drink to when they will dance, when there will be time for schmoozing, when they will listen to toasts, and when they will be able to participate in booths and activities.

I guarantee that everyone will have a better time as a result of your hard work.

Be Mindful of Guests of All Generations

While planning your event, you need to make many decisions. When you start to feel overwhelmed, keep in mind that some decisions may be optional. Just because "everyone else is doing it" doesn't mean you have to. Have the courage to not be talked into doing something that doesn't feel right to you, or that you don't feel comfortable doing.

When picking and choosing anything having to do with the event, from flowers to food to entertainment to location, your decisions should be based on how the guest will feel. Look at everything about the ceremony through their perspective and take that into account.

Your guests should feel as included as possible. Involved them in as many activities as you can, in order to make their day more special. When guests feel left out or alienated, everyone is uncomfortable, and might resort to using their cell phones to alleviate their discomfort. You want your guests to leave with the impression that they were treated with the utmost respect and made to feel important.

We received many thank you cards after my daughter's Bat Mitzvah from guests who said it was the best celebration they had ever been to. That feedback was really special to our family, because we wanted to make sure we made everyone feel included and appreciated.

Many decisions about the celebration revolve around the reception schedule. Consider the following order of events as an example:

- Cocktails

- Appetizers

- Bar or Bat Mitzvah Entrance

- Toasts

- Blessing the Bread and Wine

- Guest of Honor and Host/Hostess Dances

- Dancing the *Hora*

- Centerpiece Giveaway

- Dinner

- Candle Ceremony

- Games and Activities

- Additional Dancing

- Photos

- Dessert

We will break down the details of each aspect of the ceremony in Chapter 11 so that your guests also leave saying, "That was a fantastic party and I wish it never ended!"

As you read through the final chapters of this book, keep the guest experience in mind. Think about how each element of the celebration will feel for your different age groups.

This applies to all types of celebrations that you may host, from an afternoon luncheon to an evening event, but it is especially important if your celebration lasts for several hours, and has many moving parts. An intimate luncheon will naturally include everyone in all of the activities, whereas an evening soiree results in guests grouping and participating in activities that feel more natural to them.

Planning: Bucket Your Guests by Age Ranges

Commonly, I see that older and younger people at Bar and Bat Mitzvahs feel ignored and basically forgotten, blurred into the background. You can see it on their faces as they struggle to connect and enjoy what's going on around them.

Because it is a celebration for a teen's coming-of-age, it's easy to get lost in the idea that it's a celebration for everyone involved in the child's life and focus only on the teenagers. I witness it all the time. The music is tailored to them, as well as the games and other activities. But I know that because you picked up this planning guide, you want to avoid such a mistake.

We want to teach our children to value every generation that is present at the celebration. Judaism teaches us to do the right thing, which in this case translates into an intentional sense of giving and inclusion, making sure no one feels left out.

Since I think that data is relevant to planning and important in avoiding missteps, I encourage you to try an activity I call "bucketing your guests by age ranges."

By dividing the guests into "age buckets" (groups or categories of similarly aged attendees), you'll more clearly see the big picture demographics of who will be at the event. That will help you plan for everyone who attends, and as a result all guests will feel a sense of inclusion.

Your job as the host is to make sure that all guests have a fabulous time—not just a small subset that may account for less than 25% of the total guest list.

When you bucket your guests, you can feel empowered to plan entertainment for everyone—young and old alike, understanding how best to cater to their needs.

Start with the simple grid below and fill in the number of guests and their ages, but leave the entertainment box blank for now.

I would recommend doing this after you've sent save the date cards, but before you have sent out invitations, so that you have plenty of time to plan. A percentage of the guests included in the count may not be able to come, but that shouldn't impact the balance of ages very much.

Number of Guests	Age	Sample Entertainment
	2–10	
	11–20	
	21–40	
	41–60	
	Over 60	

Now that you have divided the potential guests by age, it's time to fill in the box under the column called "Sample Entertainment," writing down ideas that children or adults in that age range would particularly enjoy. Try to include at least two to three options in each box.

Make sure that the entertainment next to each "age bucket" has a unique value assigned to it. What follows is an example of a completed grid with the entertainment box filled in, to give you an idea of what I mean. If you want to wait and come back to fill in the entertainment after you've read Chapter 11 with its suggested activities, mark the page and come back to it.

Number of Guests	Age	Sample Entertainment
20	2–10	Magician, Caricature Artist
60	11–20	Hat Making, DJ Games
50	21–40	Vodka Ice Sculpture, Salsa Dancing
30	41–60	'80s and '90s Music, Trivia Games
20	Over 60	Baby Boomer Music, Slideshow

As you can see, the table will give you an idea how to understand the age demographics of your guests, and thereby offer appropriate entertainment so that everyone feels included and appreciated.

Going into the next two chapters with this knowledge will help you navigate the nitty-gritty planning steps to come. But before we do that, one more thing you can do to make guests comfortable.

Strategize Table Seating

Smart table seating assignments can make a world of difference for your guests' experience. Guests who know one another or have shared connections should be seated at the same table, so long as those connections and relationships are amicable. By doing so, you are making the guests feel as comfortable as possible. Most guests do not like the pressure of spending the evening with a table full of strangers—it means awkward introductions and small talk.

This rule applies to children and teenagers as well.

At my daughter's Bat Mitzvah, we seated younger guests at tables where they all had something common. For example, we had a table for the musical theater teens, the Hebrew school teens, regular school teens, and family-related teens like cousins. If you can, group all of the kid tables together and keep the adult tables separate to give the teens more autonomy.

See Chapter 7 for a reminder about my family's solution to printing our own table seating cards.

Chapter 10
Venue Selection

Start thinking about where you would like to host your Bar or
Bat Mitzvah celebration at least two years in advance.

Popular places book up quickly, especially if your event is in
the summer. You will be competing with other B'nai Mitzvot
from local synagogues, as well as weddings and all sorts of
other celebrations.

Tip

Revisit Chapter 6 on budgets if you need alternative options to the
evening celebration, either because you've waited too long and venues are
booked, or you need to look into lower-cost venues to match your budget.
Remember that the atmosphere of the venue will change according
to location and time of day, but you can host a beautiful, tasteful

celebration whether you are in a synagogue hosting a Kiddush luncheon celebration or in a ballroom hosting an evening soiree.

All of the tips and planning principles in this chapter and Chapter 11 can be altered to fit most budgets. By saving money where we could, we were able to budget for an evening at a beautiful oceanfront venue. The experiences I share of my daughter's Bat Mitzvah are largely based on a high-end celebration. But you can offer guests a similar feeling during the day in a less formal setting.

Get creative about food, entertainment, and venue, but always keep your heart and mind on the guest experience. As long as they feel included and welcomed, you're doing your job.

Remember: If you have to choose between a fancy celebration or your child's education, planning for your child's college future is more important, especially if you have multiple children to consider.

If you want to minimize your workload, both on the day of the event, and coordinating vendors ahead of time, look for an all-inclusive venue that takes care of everything, such as event setup and cleanup, audio/visual equipment, food (including appetizers, dinner, and dessert), and drinks. You may want to compare and contrast financial costs as well as the time and stress involved in coordinating many moving parts when deciding whether to go with an all-inclusive venue versus using *a la carte* vendors.

As soon as you have selected the venue, you'll need to meet with the venue coordinator to lock in prices and get clarity on the contract. At the meeting, you may need to pay a deposit, if you haven't already. Deposit percentages and refund policies can vary from venue to venue, so be sure to ask.

When you meet with the coordinator, ask for clarity on the venue's timeline as it relates to planning the celebration, and ask what the venue can do to ensure the best service and guest experience possible.

Questions to Ask

There is a lot that you need to know in order to select the right venue for your child's Bar or Bat Mitzvah. At a minimum, get answers to the following questions before you book any location. I recommend you speak with several venues to compare what they offer before you make the decision to sign a contract.

- What are the menu options and what is the deadline for selecting food? (*if the venue is all-inclusive*)

- Do they offer sample food tasting?

- Will the venue help arrange entertainment?

- Do vendors and entertainers need to be on any sort of a list to work at the event?

- When do you need to finalize the contract?

- When do you need to provide a final guest headcount?

- When is final payment due, do they offer a payment schedule, how is the fee calculated, and what form of payment do they accept?

- How will the venue deal with setup and cleanup?

- Where will the dance floor go and how many people does it accommodate? (Get the exact size dimensions.)

- Can you drop off decorations such as centerpieces ahead of time? If so, when?

- Who can you talk to on the night of the event, in case there are any issues with the service?

- Will the coordinator or a designated employee be present to help manage staff and flow?

- What sort of parking options will be available to guests and vendors?

- Will there be a coat check?

- If the venue is large enough to host more than one celebration at a time, how will they direct guests to the right place?

- How is security handled?

- How do they handle vendor setup requirements (e.g., tables, stages, chairs, power strips, etc.)?

- Do they offer extra tables and stands for gifts, table seating cards, and other items such as slide projectors, screens, and video equipment?

- How do they coordinate with outside caterers if not using an all-inclusive option?

- How will they help you with setting a schedule—and for how many hours can you book the space?

- What time will the space be available for setup and cleanup, and what time will it be available for the celebration?

- What are the "minimums" (e.g., food and drink orders, hourly fees, staff and personnel payments) that need to be met?

- How long are prices locked in for?

- Do they provide candles, tablecloths, and napkins? If so, what kind and quality?

- What type of tables and chairs are available? If you don't like the styles, can you hire an outside vendor to provide tables and chairs?

It is wise to bring this book along or write down a list of questions before you go into the meeting with the venue coordinator so you don't forget anything you wanted to ask. Also, bring along a pen and paper (or voice recorder or electronic tablet, if you prefer) to take notes. Be sure to ask the coordinator the best way to reach them in the months leading up to the celebration.

Mitzvah Packages

Ask your venue coordinator about Mitzvah packages. Many venues offer Mitzvah packages, making it easy to coordinate the evening in a way that is reflective and respectful of the spiritual and traditional Jewish nature of the event.

What follows is a list of items that Mitzvah packages often include:

- Hors d'Oeuvres

- Buffet or Plated Meal

- Challah

- Wine Service

- Dance Floor

- Table Linens and Napkins

- Candles

- Bartenders

- Maître d'

- Wait Staff

- Event Room or Ballroom

- Parking Rate Discounts

- Guest Room Accommodations (*if hotel*)

- Power Strips for the Music

- Tables and Stands for Vendors and Entertainers

- Stage for Band or DJ

- Bar

- Round Tables for Guest Seating

- Beverage and Buffet Tables

If the items above are not included in your Mitzvah package, you may need to ask for them separately or make alternate arrangements with outside vendors.

Contracts typically outline the schedule of events, along with costs. The schedule is critical to set staff expectations and ensure everything flows smoothly the evening of the event.

Venue Schedule

Once you have confirmed your venue, work together to write out a straightforward schedule of what to expect the day or evening of the event.

Include setup times, and activities that will apply to all guests: arrival, times for food and drinks, toasts and dancing.

The venue schedule does not include all of the details and intricacies of songs, games, and entertainment, which you will coordinate with your band or DJ later. Instead, it serves as a point of communication between you and the venue to determine the overarching guest needs such as food and drink, and indicate start and end times for the celebration.

Here is a sample venue schedule:

- 4:00 p.m.   Setup
- 6:00 p.m.   Guests Arrive
- 6:00 p.m.   Appetizers Served
- 6:00 p.m.   Bar Open
- 7:30 p.m.   Guests Seated
- 7:30 p.m.   Bar Closed
- 7:35 p.m.   Toasts (*10 minutes*)
- 7:45 p.m.   Dancing
- 8:15 p.m.   Dinner Served
- 9:30 p.m.   Dessert Served
- 10:00 p.m.   Bar Open
- 12:00 a.m.   Conclusion

Guest Parking

Parking should be resolved before the event. Shuttles, self-parking, valet, and rideshare services like Uber and Lyft are all options to get your guests to, from, and between the Bar or Bat Mitzvah ceremony and celebration.

If your guests plan to drive to the celebration, work with the venue coordinator to determine how to pay for valet or self-parking charges. You may choose to cover those costs, or you can have guests pay for parking. Evaluate the cost and look at your budget before you make a decision to see if it is a cost you can absorb. Whatever you decide, negotiate with the venue coordinator to see if you can get a discount on valet charges or self-parking for your guests.

Finally, communicate the parking situation to your guests. An event website is a good place to share this information. Informing your guests ahead of time is an important step in setting guest expectations. If they are expected to pay for parking, be upfront about any difference in cost between self and valet parking and let them know if they'll need cash on hand. If parking will be complimentary for guests, let them know that too. That way there are no questions.

In addition, you will need to pay for your vendors' parking. It is generally a line item written into their contracts.

Maximize the Dance Floor

One important thing to consider is the size of the dance floor. As you're looking into venues, pay attention to open space and ask about possible dance floor sizes, location, and configuration.

Avoid too tight a space, where guests end up stepping on each other. It makes for a very unpleasant guest experience. Instead, there should be plenty of room between dancers. We requested the maximum dance floor square footage in our Bat Mitzvah venue contract and they were able to accommodate us.

If you can't get enough space for your dance floor, it may be enough of a factor to prevent you from signing the venue contract. Dancing is an important part of the celebration.

Tip

If there's not enough space in the room for a large square-shaped dance floor, or if the space is wider than it is deep, you can ask about a rectangular shape instead. For example, if a room is relatively wide but the first row of dinner tables are close to the dance space, you might consider 18 ft. x 24 ft. rather than a perfectly square 20 ft. x 20 ft. dance floor. That would provide an additional two feet of space for guests to walk around the table, but you'd gain 32 sq. ft. of dance floor space.

No matter which shape you choose, make sure the dance floor will hold as many guests as possible. Keep in mind that at least 85% of the guests are on the dance floor at the beginning of the reception when the *Hora* starts and other Jewish music is played. We used a rectangle for my daughter's Bat Mitzvah, and it worked out perfectly.

Tip

If your dance floor runs on the small side, you might want to have the leader redirect guests to weave them between the tables for part of the dance.

Dance Floor Quick Reference

This following grid will give you an idea of optimal dance floor sizes, based on the number of guests.

Total Number of Guests	Total Number of Dancers	Dance Floor Size
100	50	15 ft. x 15 ft. (225 sq. ft.)
150	75	18 ft. x 18 ft. (324 sq. ft.)
200	100	20 ft. x 20 ft. (400 sq. ft.)
250	125	24 ft. x 24 ft. (576 sq. ft.)

Note:

The grid assumes a square dance floor, but total square footage is included. It also accounts for up to 50% of your guests on the dance floor, for the majority of the night, giving each dancer between 4 – 4½ square feet.

The "total number of dancers" is below the 85% mentioned above who will participate in the Hora. Group dances can be done in a more compact area since everyone will be following essentially the same moves, which diminishes the danger of bumping into each other or stepping on toes.

Guest Hotel Rooms

Once you have decided on the venue and the atmosphere of the celebration, call local hotels to see what they can offer your out-of-town guests. Ask about pricing as well as services. Do they have a gym, WiFi, pool, breakfast, or great views? You want your guests to be as comfortable as possible.

Keep in mind you are trying to make everything about the weekend convenient for your guests, so whenever possible, look for hotels that are walking distance from your venue.

It is best to give your guests at least two or three hotel options at various price points to fit their budget.

Out-of-town guests will especially appreciate locations near a mall or city hub. That way they can have something to do in between events, like watch a movie or go shopping.

If you live near a beautiful outdoor space (such as a beach or mountain), guests will also appreciate a hotel with a view they wouldn't see at home—especially if there are walking trails or outdoor recreational activities available.

Tip

You may wish to reread and review the section on reserving hotel blocks in Chapter 4, listed under "12 Months Before the Event."

Additional Contracts to Sign

Beyond the venue, the number of contracts you sign will depend on how elaborate your event is and how many vendors you plan to hire.

Here are just a few of the potential vendors mentioned in this book:

- Photographer

- Videographer

- Band or DJ

- Magician

- Caricature Artist

- Photo Booth

- Caterer

Be prepared to sign a lot of contracts. Most, if not all, will require a deposit. Entertainment and hotel vendors will require this before they agree to handle your event.

Following are some of the elements typically included in vendor contracts:

- Event Details: date, location, duration, schedule, and services rendered

- Pricing: itemized calculations, service charges, taxes, gratuity, minimum fees, and total costs

- Parking: self or valet

- Meals: food and non-alcoholic drinks

- Disclaimers

- Payment Methods and Schedules

- Equipment Requirements: e.g., stage sizes and amplifier hookups

- Cancellation Policies

If you have any questions about the terms of the contract, reach out to your venue coordinator or vendor and ask for clarification. They will agree that it is best to have everyone on the same page.

Tip

Keep track of all of your contracts. It helps to have both a digital and printed version, so that you can view contracts on your computer, but also have folders and schedules for easy access offline.

You may want to have these handy on the day of the event, along with each vendor's contact information, so that you can call them if there are any issues or last-minute adjustments that arise.

Pay close attention to payment due dates and any steps required to fulfill and finalize the contract, such as guest counts or order details.

Contract Negotiation

When you are signing contracts, know that all items are negotiable. See if they can discount anything, from the venue to guest hotel parking fees, guest room rates, gift bag delivery, and food and beverages. If the reception is at a hotel, they might even throw in a complimentary room for you on the night of the event.

Negotiable items with entertainment vendors may include vendor meals and parking, payment schedules, and pricing.

Remember, you have nothing to lose by asking if services can be discounted.

Tip

Before signing a contract, agree on the arrival and departure times as well as meals and break times for each of your vendors, including your photographer and videographer, band or DJ, and all of your entertainers.

Chapter 11
The Celebration

Hopefully, by now we've convinced you that the best Bar or Bat Mitzvah is planned with your guests in mind. There are several elements to think about when planning the celebration, each important to a well-rounded event.

Many of the sections in this chapter are catered to the idea of an evening celebration. However, even if you are hosting an afternoon gathering or smaller event, there are elements that you may want to consider. While meals and entertainment may be less elaborate, creative activities for kids and teens and a mindful approach to weaving Jewish traditions into the celebration will always be appreciated.

Celebration Schedule

As a reminder, here is the list of events and activities to figure into the schedule, as presented in Chapter 9. We will go through each in depth during this chapter.

- Cocktails

- Appetizers

- Bar or Bat Mitzvah Entrance

- Toasts

- Blessing the Bread and Wine

- Guest of Honor and Host/Hostess Dances

- *Hora*

- Centerpiece Giveaway

- Meal

- Candle Lighting Ceremony

- Games and Activities

- Dancing

- Photos

- Dessert

On a separate piece of paper, you may wish to draw a grid, with the hours of the Bar or Bat Mitzvah celebration along the left side, broken down into chunks. You may wish to plan it out to every half hour of the celebration, or expand it to only represent major shifts in activity.

Make a rectangle for each "chunk," or section of time. As you go through the chapter, fill in that rectangle with applicable food, dancing, and activities.

Here is a rough example, illustrating a couple of hours of a sample celebration schedule.

Time	Food / Drink	Activity
7:00–8:00	Cocktail Bar and Appetizers	Magician, Schmoozing, Hat Making
8:00-8:30	Bar Closed	Toasts, Blessings, Jewish Dances, Centerpiece Giveaway
8:30–9:30	Dinner Served, Soft Drinks, Wine	Teens: Headphone Games with DJ, Trivia Competitions
9:30-10:30	Coffee, Tea, Dessert	Caricature Artist, Hat Making, Candle Lighting Ceremony, Dancing
10:30-11:30	Bar Open, Snacks and Cordials	Professional Dance Lesson, Dancing and Schmoozing

Some things, like the entrance and the blessing of the bread and wine, will be clearly marked for a specific time. Other things, like the bar, or interactive activity booths such as crafts, will cover several sections.

This will help you visualize the evening. You will be able to quickly identify times that every guest's attention will be on the same activity (e.g., the *Hora*, toasts, candle lighting ceremony, dinner, and centerpiece giveaway), and times that guests will have several options to choose from (e.g., dancing, caricatures, schmoozing, etc.).

You can refer to the venue schedule in Chapter 10 for a general timeline of the primary activities of the evening, such as the cocktail hour, meal, toasts, and dancing.

I highly recommend you work with your DJ or bandleader as you are figuring out the schedule, and make sure they have a final copy of all of the moving parts.

They are experienced in keeping a celebration moving, so rely on their expertise and advice to put together a cohesive event. Every hour should be planned out in detail to keep the flow intact. This helps set the expectations for everyone at the event including service crews and guests.

Make sure each vendor or entertainer has a schedule that applies specifically to them so that they know what is expected without having to look through a complicated document with intricate details and schedules.

The exception is your DJ or bandleader, who should have a schedule of everything. They will be able to direct and announce events as they are scheduled to occur and keep guests entertained and informed, leaving you to visit and enjoy the evening.

Entrance or Toast

Work with your DJ or bandleader to decide how you want to enter the celebration. Some people choose to make a big entrance after the cocktail hour has already started. Others prefer to greet guests as they arrive, and officially kick off the celebration with a toast.

Ultimately, the decision is yours, and there may be a way to do both, but please do take into consideration the spirit of honoring your guests and the spirituality of the celebration as you decide how to handle it.

Make an Entrance

If you choose to make an entrance after the cocktail hour has gotten underway, work with your DJ or bandleader to determine the best time to do it.

Making an entrance means that the nuclear family of the Bar or Bat Mitzvah will be officially announced by the DJ or bandleader as they enter the reception area.

Generally, the parents are introduced first, then any siblings, and lastly the Bar or Bat Mitzvah boy or girl.

On occasion, I have seen entrances that surpass the red carpet at the Academy Awards. Although you are free to choose what works best for your family and your event, I will say that I am not a big fan of over-the-top grand entrances. I find them inconsistent with the ceremonial values of modesty and humility that have been reaffirmed earlier that morning during the service.

To avoid an air of narcissism, and keep the focus on the religious sanctity of the day, if you choose to make a grand entrance, I advise you to tone it down. At my daughter's Bat Mitzvah, we decided to forgo any kind of grand entrance and opted for a toast instead.

If you have an open conversation with your DJ or bandleader about a balanced approach, they should be able to help you make an entrance that is tasteful and joyous.

Celebrate Guests With A Toast

One alternative to a grand entrance that still acknowledges the Bar or Bat Mitzvah and introduces the family is to give a toast.

A toast can be classy, and guests appreciate the age-old tradition. It is a time to give thanks to guests and share a warm story about the child they are all there to support and celebrate.

At my daughter's Bat Mitzvah, my husband gave a small welcome speech to the guests as well as a congratulatory message to our daughter. Many guests came to me later and said it was a refreshing approach.

The toast can be simple and might start off something like this:

"Congratulations to (*the Bat Mitzvah child*) on your special day. This is a celebration of life! We are very happy that our friends and family could celebrate this monumental event with us. We also want to welcome all of the out-of-town guests who traveled far in order to share this special day with us!"

Then also add how special and meaningful the day is and thank the guests for coming including a special thank you to all relatives and out-of-town guests.

The toasts should end by raising a glass and saying "Mazel Tov," which is the traditional saying to the Bar and Bat Mitzvah child, family and even guests. *Mazel Tov* translates to "good destiny," but it is now used universally as the Jewish equivalent of "Congratulations." You can even follow the toast with a song like "L'Chaim" from *Fiddler on the Roof*.

Spiritual and Traditional Blessings

There are several ways to incorporate spiritual and traditional touches in your child's Bar or Bat Mitzvah celebration. Jewish guests will appreciate keeping the traditions alive and the tone and atmosphere that traditions convey, and non-Jewish guests will love to have an intimate look at Judaism.

It creates quite a special ambiance for guests, the feeling of experiencing traditions that have been commonplace for hundreds of years.

Candle Lighting Ceremony

The purpose of a candle lighting ceremony is to honor relatives and out-of-town guests. Although we did not include a candle lighting ceremony at my daughter's Bat Mitzvah, I highly recommend it as a way to make the celebration more meaningful. The tradition is a wonderful way to honor special guests and show respect.

Anytime you embrace an opportunity to make your guests feel special, you are on the right track.

Here are some guidelines to consider when planning a candle lighting ceremony.

• Decide how many candles to light: 8–14 are typical.

• Choose who will be invited to come forward and light each candle. This honor is generally given to close family members and friends.

• Plan out the order in which people you will be called up to light their candle. The ceremony usually starts with honored elders, and ends with friends and immediate family. Here is one recommended sequence: grandparents, aunts, uncles, cousins, older relatives, younger relatives, family friends, the child's friends, siblings, and parents.

• You'll need to select music for the ceremony. Generally, one song is played for each candle lit, but speak with your DJ or bandleader to decide what best fits the time and flow specific to your child's celebration. A Google search for "candle lighting songs" will give you some great ideas.

- Have your Bar or Bat Mitzvah child take a few minutes to write about the special people invited to light the candles. You can help them with this task. Sometimes it helps spur ideas to have a format, such as a rhyming quatrain or couplet. The tone does not have to be serious. It is okay to include both touching and humorous details about your honorees. For example: "I love when you take me shopping all over town. We buy clothes or just walk around. You are extremely important to me, so Grandma and Grandpa, with all my love, please light candle three."

The candle lighting ceremony is a true honor, and everyone chosen will remember it for life. Other guests will be glad to know the Bar or Bat Mitzvah's closest relatives and friends and share in their moment.

Blessings for Wine, Bread, and *Havdalah*

Traditional Jewish blessings over the food are another way to incorporate tradition and foster a reverent atmosphere. Here are the blessings for wine and bread, and the *Havdalah* ceremony.

Wine Blessing (*Kiddush*)

The *Kiddush* is recited over a full cup of wine or grape juice. *Kiddush* occurs just before blessing the bread (*HaMotzi*), and can be done by either of the Mitzvah's parents or a friend or relative of the family.

בָּרוּךְ אַתָּה יְיָ, אֱלֹהֵינוּ מֶלֶךְ הָעוֹלָם, בּוֹרֵא פְּרִי הַגָּפֶן.

Baruch ata Adonai, Eloheinu melech ha-olam, borei p'ri hagafen.

Translation: Blessed are You, Lord, Our G-d, King of the Universe, Who creates fruit of the vine.

Bread Blessing (*HaMotzi*)

After the Kiddush, the *HaMotzi* is recited to bless the challah.

בָּרוּךְ אַתָּה יְיָ אֱלֹהֵינוּ מֶלֶךְ הָעוֹלָם, הַמּוֹצִיא לֶחֶם מִן הָאָרֶץ

Baruch ata Adonai Eloheinu, melekh ha'olam, hamotzi lehem min ha'aretz.

Translation: Blessed are You, Lord our Gd, King of the Universe, Who brings forth bread from the earth.

Havdalah Ceremony

If you are hosting a Saturday night reception, performing the *Havdalah* could be a huge hit. *Havdalah* is a "mini-service" marking the end of the Jewish Sabbath. It is quite simple to perform, with only four blessings—wine, spices, candle, and a couple of prayers marking the end of the *Sabbath*. But the impact is powerful.

To perform the ceremony, you will need:

- *Havdalah* candle (braided multi-wick candle) and candle holder

- Cup (filled with wine or grape juice)

- Container of sweet-smelling spices (cinnamon or cloves)

Overhead lights are usually dimmed or turned off so that only the *Havdalah* candle produces light.

Blessings are recited over the wine, then over the spices, which are passed around for everyone to smell the 'sweetness' of the departing *Sabbath*.

Finally, the candle is blessed and lifted for all to see. Guests raise and reach their hands toward the candle as if feeling the warmth of the *Sabbath*.

Between the low lighting, the flicker of the *Havdalah* candle, the sweet-smelling *Havdalah* spices, and the blessings which are sung, it can be quite a gorgeous highlight to the start of the evening.

If you decide to perform *Havdalah*, you may want to include a small bag of cinnamon and other cloves on each table so they can be passed around to all guests during the blessing over the spices.

Below is a simplified version of the blessings, transliterations, and translations for you to perform this ritual. For a full version of *Havdalah*, including songs that follow, visit *My Jewish Learning* (www.myjewishlearning.com/article/havdalah-taking-leave-of-shabbat).

The Blessing over Wine or Grape Juice

בָּרוּךְ אַתָּה יְיָ, אֱלֹהֵינוּ מֶלֶךְ הָעוֹלָם, בּוֹרֵא פְּרִי הַגָּפֶן

Transliteration: *Baruch atah, Adonai, Elohaynu melech ha'olam, boray pri hagafen.*

Translation: Blessed are You, G-d, our Lord, King of the universe, Creator of the fruit of the vine.

The Blessing over Spices

בָּרוּךְ אַתָּה יְיָ, אֱלֹהֵינוּ מֶלֶךְ הָעוֹלָם, בּוֹרֵא מִינֵי בְשָׂמִים

Transliteration: *Baruch atah, Adonai, Elohaynu melech ha'olam, boray minay vesamim.*

Translation: Blessed are You, G-d, our Lord, King of the universe, Creator of the different spices.

The Blessing over the Candle

בָּרוּךְ אַתָּה יְיָ, אֱלֹהֵינוּ מֶלֶךְ הָעוֹלָם, בּוֹרֵא מְאוֹרֵי הָאֵשׁ

Transliteration: *Baruch atah, Adonai, Elohaynu melech ha'olam, bo-ray me'oray ha'aysh.*

Translation: Blessed are You, G-d, our Lord, King of the universe, Creator of the fire's lights.

The Blessing over *Havdalah*

בָּרוּךְ אַתָּה יְיָ, אֱלֹהֵינוּ מֶלֶךְ הָעוֹלָם, הַמַּבְדִּיל בֵּין קֹדֶשׁ
לְחוֹל, בֵּין אוֹר לְחֹשֶׁךְ, בֵּין יִשְׂרָאֵל לָעַמִּים, בֵּין יוֹם הַשְּׁבִיעִי
לְשֵׁשֶׁת יְמֵי הַמַּעֲשֶׂה. בָּרוּךְ אַתָּה יְיָ, הַמַּבְדִּיל בֵּין קֹדֶשׁ לְחוֹל

Transliteration: *Baruch atah, Adonai, Elohaynu melech ha'ol-am, hamavdil bayn kodesh lechol bayn or lechoshechbayn Yisrael la'amim bayn yom hashevi'i leshayshet yemay hama'aseh. Baruch atah, Adonai, hamavdil bayn kodesh lechol.*

Translation: Blessed are You, G-d, our Lord, King of the universe, who separates between the holy and the profane; between the light and dark; between Israel and the other nations; between the seventh day and the six days of the week. Blessed are You, G-d, who separates between the holy and the profane.

Birkat Hamazon

Birkat Hamazon is most commonly known as the blessing after the meal. This traditional ritual is generally performed in Orthodox and some Conservative circles and signifies the end of the festive meal. You can hand out booklets of prayers, called *benchers*, to guests who would like to join you in reciting the prayers.

Food Selections

There are essentially three parts to food service at any formal or evening event: appetizers, entrées, and desserts. If you are planning a daytime celebration, you may be able to forgo appetizers, but be sure to include desserts.

When you're sending your final counts to the caterer, pay close attention to the age groups that you defined in Chapter 9. They will need to know the ratio of children and teen meals to adult meals.

Beyond your guests and your family, you will need to provide a meal for your vendors. If catering through your venue, they will have specific rates dedicated for vendor meals. A typical vendor meal might be chicken and pasta. This meal will generally cost less than your guest meals. Speak with your venue about where vendors can sit for their meals and arrange separate tables and/or rooms to accommodate them.

Keep To Kosher Style

Your level of Kosher observance at the ceremony will depend on your family and your guests. Even if most of your guests are not Kosher, it may be considered poor taste by some to serve obviously non-Kosher food such as pork and shellfish products. For example, you may wish to avoid some of the following appetizers commonly offered by event venues and caterers: shrimp cocktail, lobster sushi, stuffed crab, anything with pork in it.

There are plenty of food options for Kosher-style or Kosher-certified food that taste delicious.

If a specific meal or appetizer that you want to serve has elements that are not Kosher, you may wish to ask your caterer if they can alter or substitute the recipe for your Bar or Bat Mitzvah celebration.

Remember, the goal is to establish consistency between the ceremony and the reception, so Kosher options are of great importance.

All of the foods I suggest in this book can be considered Kosher-friendly. Be sure there are ample selections for guests who observe *Kashrut* traditions and ask the venue or outside caterer to read the following guidelines carefully. For observant guests, you will need to have Kosher meals delivered to the premises, since their meals must be prepared at establishments that adhere to strict *Kashrut* standards and require Kosher rabbinical supervision.

Kosher Style Food Guidelines

Here are few basic Kosher style food guidelines:

- Only certain animals are Kosher (cows, sheep, chicken, turkey). Pig is not. To be Kosher, animals are supposed to be slaughtered in a ritual manner, and blessed by a Rabbi.

- Only certain sea animals with scales and fins are Kosher (most fish, no shellfish).

- Meat and dairy products are not served at the same meal.

Tip

Even if most guests are not Kosher, be sensitive to those who are. Check with your more religious guests to find out what they will be most comfortable eating. Some will be fine with vegetarian or fish options, while others will prefer Glatt Kosher meals that need to be delivered to their tables from an outside vendor that follows strict Kashrut laws.

Advance research will ensure everyone can partake in your simcha (celebration).

Your caterer or event coordinator can guide you in selecting a menu that will work for your guests, within your budget. Set aside time to sample some of the foods and to help you make a decision.

Appetizers

Variety keeps things interesting and ensures there will be something that everyone can enjoy. Offer at least six or seven different types of appetizers so that guests will be continually surprised.

There are generally two styles of service to choose from: tray-passed appetizers or reception stations.

If choosing tray-passed appetizers, choose options that will appeal to the majority of your guests.

Be sure to offer a handful of vegetarian options, as everyone can enjoy them.

Tray-Passed Appetizers

These are bite-size appetizers circulated by your wait staff. They add a formal touch to any celebration, and guests love to discover their options as wait staff walk by. Tray-passed appetizers allow guests to stand (or sit) and visit while the food comes to them. There is no line, and the appetizers always look plentiful as new trays are constantly coming out.

Sample tray-passed appetizers might include:

- Ahi Tuna with Wonton Crisps

- Pear and Gorgonzola Canapes

- Fruit and Cheese Platters

- Smoked Salmon Blini

- Duck Pâté and Crackers

- Roasted Eggplant

- Grilled Portobello Mushrooms

- Grilled Chicken with Pesto

- Beef Teriyaki Skewers

- Grilled Vegetables

- Bruschetta

- Vegetable Spring Rolls

- Assorted Sushi (*Kosher* fish only)

- Chicken or Beef Pot Stickers

- Beef Sliders

Reception Stations

Consider reception stations as an alternative to tray-passed appetizers. They allow guests to regulate the quantity and selection of appetizers they prefer and reduce wait staff needed during the cocktail hour. These can be used instead of, or in addition to, tray-passed appetizers.

Each station can have foods grouped on platters, which allows for more variety than tray-passed appetizers. Sample reception stations might include:

- Crudité with Grilled and Raw Vegetables

- Meat Platters

- Smoked Salmon with Capers, Onion, Egg, and Chives on Toasted Bread

- Cheese with Crackers

- Baguette, Dried Fruits, and Roasted Nuts

- Assorted Sushi (Kosher only): Salmon, Ahi, California Roll (Use Imitation Crab), Spicy Tuna Roll

- Sliced Fruits and Berries

Tip

A couple of notes on sushi: I advise you order the extra large platter because it tends to be popular, especially in Southern California where we live. For my daughter's Bat Mitzvah, we ordered one hundred pieces, and they were gone within minutes. Also, remember that Kosher style means skipping shellfish. Imitation crab is a good substitute for real crab. Most fish are okay as long as it has fins and scales.

Appetizers with a Twist

If you want to wow your guests with appetizer and drink combinations (alcoholic and non-alcoholic), here are a few unique pairings:

- Margarita Shooters with Mini Spicy Tuna Tacos

- Arnold Palmer Shooters with Chicken and Grits

- Beer Shooters with Beef Pigs-in-a-Blanket

- Hot Tomato Soup with Parmesan-Crusted Toast

And for after dinner snacks:

- Cookie Chasers with Shots of Milk

Tip

If you choose reception stations, make sure your guests know that entrees will follow. If you plan to host a buffet-style dinner, and therefore did not include a meal order on your RSVPs, guests may not know that you intend to serve a full dinner after heavy appetizers.

At one Bar Mitzvah I attended, there were seven reception stations, each with a unique cuisine.

An entire room was dedicated to appetizers, spread across seven stations: Chinese, Italian, French, American, Thai, Japanese, and Mexican. An hour later, a bell rang and we moved into another room where we were served an extensive three-course sit-down meal. I was already full! If I had known, I would have paced myself.

Entrees

Just as there are two main options for how to serve appetizers, there are two main options for the main course as well: the buffet and the sit-down dinner. I recommend a hybrid of the two.

The trend is buffet service for the teens and a sit-down meal for adults.

Although you can choose buffet style for the adults, I find a sit-down dinner is more relaxing for your guests.

Meal Service for Kids and Teens

Kids and teens love to fill up their own plate with the foods that they like, on their own time. The option to return for seconds of a favorite food also appeals to teens.

That is why I recommend the buffet approach to feeding kids of all ages. It is less formal than a sit-down service, and they will appreciate the flexibility and ownership of choosing how to balance their meal. Plus, with only a portion of the guests eating at the buffet, lines will be manageable.

Some popular teen buffet foods include:

- Macaroni and Cheese

- Baked Ziti Marinara

- Hamburgers

- Kosher Hot Dogs

- Chicken Fingers

- Meatballs

- French Fries

- Corn on the Cob

- Carrot and Celery Sticks

- Beef in Blankets

- Breaded Mozzarella Sticks

Meal Service for Adults

While kids and teens will enjoy socializing in a buffet line and plating their own food, I lean against it for adult guests. Instead, if you are able, arrange for a sit-down meal for the adults, served by wait staff.

Sit-down meals create a calm, relaxed ambience for adult guests, and the goal is to make them feel as relaxed and comfortable as possible. Instead of waiting in long lines, guests will be able to allocate more of their time toward socializing. You've worked hard at table seating arrangements, making sure that guests seated together have a shared connection. They will prefer to spend time schmoozing, rather than waiting for direction on which table goes next and wondering how long it will take for the line to move. Generally speaking, most people do not like to stand in lines.

While they are waiting for table service, they'll be able to sit, schmooze, and enjoy bread and a beverage.

While buffet and a sit-down service may ultimately take the same amount of time for everyone to get their food and to eat, the sit-down service will feel less rushed. Slowing down the pace of the event is a good thing and will bring more enjoyment to everyone involved.

When you are planning your child's Bar or Bat Mitzvah celebration, you will need to offer adults at least three different entrée options: a vegetarian dish, a fish dish, and a chicken or beef dish.

Here are some sit-down dinner meal options that I find cover all of your guests' preferences. Work with your venue or caterer to select the three meals according to their menu.

- Boneless Chicken Francaise and Pureed Cauliflower

- Red Snapper with Lime Beurre Blanc Sauce and Lemon Asparagus

- Apricot Orange-Glazed French Chicken and Baby Carrots

- Baked Salmon Fillet with Champagne Sauce and Grilled Vegetables

- Oven Roasted Beef Tenderloin and Garlic Mashed Potatoes

- Roast Prime Rib Au Jus and Truffle Mashed Potatoes

- Grilled Marinated Tofu and Roasted Sweet Potato Hash

- Chicken Pasta with Grilled Vegetables

- Seared Pacific Sea Bass with Roasted Artichokes & Tomatoes

- Seared Steak Fillet with Béarnaise Sauce and Roasted Potatoes

I highly recommend serving adult guests salad before the main meal. Even if your entrée includes vegetables on the plate, a salad is a nice touch and adds an element of formality with multiple courses.

Whether you include the salad or not, each meal should include vegetables, fresh bread and butter, and coffee and tea.

Dessert

Be sure to offer something sweet after dinner. Again, I recommend a hybrid between buffet for the kids and teens and sit-down service for the adults.

Kid and Teen Dessert

Just as children and teens will enjoy serving themselves a buffet dinner, they'll love Do-It-Yourself desserts. Anytime you can incorporate a fun and creative activity to the schedule, the teens will love it.

Ask if your venue offers chocolate fountains and ice cream sundae stations. Many do, and they are always a hit.

For the chocolate fountain, we were able to pick five toppings from the following list:

- Strawberries

- Oreo Cookies

- Pretzels

- Brownies

- Rice Crispy Treats

- Marshmallows

- Bananas

- Pineapple Chunks

- Cookies

- Macaroons

- Cheesecake

We also offered ice cream sundae stations with the following toppings:

- Chocolate Fudge

- Sprinkles

- Cookie Crumbles

- Chopped Nuts

- M&Ms

- Whipped Cream

As you can see in the photo, the stations were a lot of fun, and the teens loved playing dessert chef for the evening.

Adult Dessert

Since you may only be able to offer one or two dessert selections for your adult sit-down dinner guests, choose dessert that you feel the majority will enjoy. Ask your caterer or venue coordinator for ideas and recommendations.

We ended up picking a chocolate dessert because most people like chocolate, even though some people would rather have fruit in their dessert. Maybe a compromise is possible with a fruit garnish on the plate.

Some desserts that you might want to think about are:

- Apple Tarts

- New York Cheesecake

- Chocolate Lava Cake

- Chocolate Ganache

- Tiramisu

- Fruit Tart

Drinks

When planning drinks, there are several things to consider, and each guest will likely consume several beverages throughout the evening.

For an afternoon gathering or restaurant luncheon, water, sodas, lemonade, iced tea, coffee, and tea will suffice. These are drinks normally found on any menu. You can order pitchers, or have guests make individual requests.

An evening gathering should include all of the above, and may also include alcoholic beverages and non-alcoholic (or virgin) cocktails. You may wish to include beer and wine only, or offer hard liquor and mixed drinks as well. Furthermore, alcoholic service can be offered throughout the evening or only during certain hours, and you can choose whether to cover the cost of all beverages or only a certain number or type of drinks and offer a cash bar for the rest.

As you can see, deciding how to handle drinks can get extremely complicated and there is a lot to consider.

Let's examine the options.

Alcoholic Beverages

When it comes to serving the 21-and-over crowd, your venue coordinator will need to know how long you want the bar to be open, and whether you want it to be host or no-host.

It is widely recommended that the bar be open during cocktail hour while appetizers are served, closed during dinner, and open again after dessert.

Host vs. No-Host Bar

A host bar is an open bar, where the host pays for all of the drinks. Venues may charge by the hour, by the bottle, by the drink, or per person. If you can fit it into your budget, we recommend you opt for the host bar.

A no-host bar means guests pay for their drinks. Choose a no-host bar if you have limited funds.

Note that charges often vary between host and no-host bars. A no-host bar often costs one to two dollars more per drink, to make up for the bartender's additional time and effort collecting money.

If your budget is somewhere in the middle, it's important to note that host bars can be limit or no limit. You have the option to limit the number of drinks sold. One way to handle this as the host is to give vouchers to guests for a limited number of free drinks. Once they've used up their vouchers, guests pay cash for any additional drinks they order. This can go against proper etiquette standards, so I recommend avoiding vouchers unless you have to be particularly budget-conscious.

This only applies to alcoholic or specialty beverages. Water, soda, coffee, and tea should always be made free and available to all guests.

For my daughter's Bat Mitzvah, we opted for a host bar with no limit, serving premium brands for cordials, hard liquor, cognacs, beer, and wine.

Soft drinks and sparkling and bottled waters were also available at the bar.

Tip

Some venues require you to meet minimum beverage amounts in order to provide bar service. If yours does, I suggest you upgrade your drinks to the highest quality brands available to meet the minimum. That ensures you won't be paying more for drinks than you ordered. These minimum orders will be noted in your event contract. For example, if the venue has a $3000 minimum bar order, and you only order $2100 worth, you'll still be charged for the full $3000. That can feel like wasted money.

We upgraded to the Deluxe Brands Bar Package since otherwise we would have fallen short of our required minimum fee.

You can also meet your minimums by ordering an abundance of wine and champagne and taking home the leftover wine. Before you select this as an option, make sure the contract that you signed allows you take home unopened bottles.

It can be fun to save a few extra bottles to celebrate special occasions down the road, such as when your Bar or Bat Mitzvah turns twenty-one, graduates from college, gets engaged, and so on.

Alcoholic Beverage Quality and Pricing

Prices are determined based on quality and brand. I've included a detailed breakdown of beverages to help guide you through the decision-making process.

First, your venue will ask you to decide between lower-end and higher-end alcohol brands. Our venue grouped the liquor into four different bar packages. I include whiskey brand names to give you an idea of the quality at each level.

Well Brands: lower-end vodka, gin, tequila, rum, bourbon and whiskey (Canadian Club)

Call Brands: same spirits, but a step up in terms of quality (Seagram's 7)

Premium Brands: same spirits, but another step up (Jameson)

Deluxe Brands: same spirits, cream of the crop (Crown Royal)

Sliding pricing scales are created based on the Brand Bar Package chosen.

Sample Bar Packages

Your venue coordinator or caterer will provide you with options for bar packages. These are examples of options and pricing you may see.

Well Brands Package: well brands, wine, domestic and imported beers, soft drinks, bottled and sparkling water, juice ($10 per person first hour, $6 per person each additional hour)

Call Brands Package: call brands, wine, domestic and imported beers, soft drinks, bottled and sparkling water, juice ($13 per person first hour, $9 per person each additional hour)

Premium Brands Package: premium brands, wine, domestic and imported beers, soft drinks, bottled and sparkling water, juice ($17 per person first hour, $13 per person each additional hour)

Deluxe Brands Package: deluxe brands, wine, domestic and imported beers, soft drinks, bottled and sparkling water, juice ($20 per person first hour, $15 per person each additional hour)

After-dinner drinks (cordials such as Grand Marnier and cognacs such as Courvoisier) are also included in bar packages.

Wine is typically served at the table. Your venue will offer a choice of reds and whites for you to select. If your contract requires that you meet a minimum drink charge, as was our case, I recommend that you upgrade your wine to the highest quality.

Bar Set-Up Fee

In addition to drinks, you will probably be charged an attended bar set-up fee. Be prepared for this expense. Rates vary but may run around $150–200 per bar.

Special Non-Alcoholic Drinks for Kids and Teens

Beverages for children and teens are usually included in the price of the buffet unless specified. Typical teen beverages might include lemonade, fruit punch, or sodas. At my daughter's Bat Mitzvah, we also purchased a fancy ice sculpture fountain filled with root beer for the kids (*photo and description later in the chapter*). It was a fun decorative element and it intrigued our guests.

Decorations

Even if your venue already looks festive, think about how you can make the room look and feel more special. Be prepared to bring in centerpieces, plus any flowers, balloons, photos and posters that you'd like to display. Also, work with the venue coordinator on tablecloth and napkin quality and colors, and ask the band or DJ if they plan to bring any special lighting to amp up the dance floor, but avoid overdoing it since you want to maintain a celebratory atmosphere, rather than a party atmosphere with strobe lights.

If you are hosting the celebration at a restaurant or synagogue, work with their staff to find out how you can make the space feel special for a tasteful Bar or Bat Mitzvah celebration.

Creative Centerpieces

Centerpieces are a great way to think outside the box, break tradition, and allow your Bar or Bat Mitzvah teen to express him or herself.

Of course, flowers are always a beautiful option and the most traditional approach to centerpieces, but you can save money and leave a memorable impression by mixing it up.

We had decided against a theme for the reasons shared in Chapter 3, but it was important to my daughter and me that we take that time that would have been spent on planning the theme, to make creative centerpieces instead that kept to the theme of her *Tikkun Olam* Mitzvah project. It ended up being a wonderful activity to share with my Bat Mitzvah daughter.

We had fun planning and designing something special for the guests.

To make the centerpieces, we went to a local art store and bought peacock feathers, wooden birdhouses, and stuffed animals. Each table was named for the stuffed animal in its centerpiece. We had eighteen tables, so we had to find eighteen unique stuffed animals!

Even with all of the components, our creative centerpieces turned out to be very inexpensive compared to quotes we got from our local florists.

Once we had purchased and designed the elements and hand-painted the birdhouses, we negotiated with a local grocery store to combine our peacock feathers and birdhouses with a bouquet of real flowers that they provided. These items were arranged in sturdy square containers (provided by the store) to produce a lovely centerpiece.

They were able to assemble the centerpieces with the table seating cards, as well as the stuffed animals used to identify table names and assignments. They did a great job and even delivered the centerpieces to the reception that evening. Our guests were pleasantly surprised by the arrangements.

The biggest benefit for us was a beautiful mother-daughter memory. I bonded with my daughter as we meticulously painted each birdhouse. Each time we would go shopping and stumble on a new animal for our centerpiece collection, we'd get a thrill. Every new animal we discovered (e.g., walrus, turtle, sea lion, giraffe, cheetah, monkey) felt like we hit the jackpot.

This was not a time-saver. But it was time well spent. Even though we spent many hours painting the birdhouses and shopping for animals and it took us many months to complete, we felt we were accomplishing something worthwhile.

Whether it's the centerpieces or some other element of design and decoration, I highly recommend that you think of something to do with your teenager that involves them in the planning and brings out your creative side at the same time.

Tip

Start early if you plan on making your own centerpieces.

Additional Centerpiece Ideas

The options truly are endless. We've seen many beautiful centerpieces at celebrations we've attended and seen lovely photos online. Here are a few options and photos that might interest you: photo cubes, seashells, bamboo arrangements, glass beads, glowing beads, and goldfish.

Blue Glass Vase Centerpiece photo: www.occasionsbyshangrila.com

Do-It-Yourself (DIY) centerpieces can be very inexpensive and budget-friendly. All you need is an idea and some dedication to make them. Use Pinterest to search for incredible Bar and Bat Mitzvah centerpiece ideas. There is a link to Mitzvah ideas on Pinterest in the resources section of the book.

Ice Sculptures

This is a photo of the root beer sculpture mentioned earlier in the chapter. We got the idea thanks to a friend's event.

We had attended a gorgeous Bar Mitzvah where there was a four-foot ice sculpture on display. The ice sculpture acted as a luge where the attendant poured and served the guests vodka.

We were so mesmerized and impressed that I decided to buy one for my daughter's Bat Mitzvah. Guests young and old were fascinated by carved ice doubling as a drink luge, and it was the first time that many had seen such a sculpture. Fortunately, our venue had worked with ice sculpture vendors before and was able to recommend a good vendor. You can also Google local vendors and be sure to read reviews when selecting one.

Tip

If you decide to include ice sculpture in your decorations and the budget allows for two, consider getting one for the adults and one for the teens.

The adult sculpture can be used to serve some type of hard liquor like vodka.

The teen sculpture can be used for a non-alcoholic drink that is fun and festive, such as lemonade, soda, or fruit punch.

We opted for a single root beer ice sculpture since we didn't want to have multiple ice sculptures. We were worried that if we provided the adults with a liquor-filled one, there might be too much alcohol and we wanted to keep the celebration upbeat.

Slideshow and Video Presentations

At the reception, we recommend you give guests the option to view the photo slideshow and video montage—or not.

A mandatory slideshow and/or video montage stops the continuous flow of party, which you want to avoid. While slideshows are popular and many guests will love to look at old photos, there will be a handful of guests who may be bored by the experience. Avoid a scenario where all guests are obligated to watch thirty to forty minutes of baby pictures.

The best method is to have an ongoing slideshow in the background, running on a loop from the moment the guests arrive to the moment they depart. That way guests can choose if and when to watch and work it organically into their experience.

Pictures should show in chronological order, starting with baby pictures and working your way up through the years.

Remember that the message you want to convey throughout the Bar or Bat Mitzvah celebration is one of inclusion and consideration. Honor your guests by including them in as many slideshow photos as you can, so they will feel appreciated.

One side benefit of a slideshow running throughout the event is that you can avoid the question of how many photos to include, and how long to make the slideshow. You can put as many or as few photos as you like since your coverage will last the entire event. If the slideshow loops, guests can tune in and out of the show, knowing that if they miss a photo, there will be another chance to view it.

Tip

Pause or turn off the slideshow or video montage during toasts, blessings, and traditional Jewish dances to keep all of the attention on the group activity. If it is in a locations that won't distract your guests from other activities, you can keep it running.

Slideshow Software and Photo Selection

Making a slideshow can be time-consuming, but it is not difficult. You should be able to make one on your home computer using built-in media programs, so there is no need to buy special software. If you have a PC, check out Microsoft's Windows Media Program. Mac users can use iMovie or iPhoto. If you want something fancier, a web search can turn up several free and paid options.

As noted in the timeline, I recommend that you start this task several months before the celebration because of the time involved. The content is entirely up to you, as long as you keep it pleasant and tasteful.

Background instrumental music is available within slideshow software, or you can choose music that is meaningful to your Bar or Bat Mitzvah.

Tip

In addition to family photos in your possession, invite friends and extended family to submit photos that they have with the Bar or Bat Mitzvah. This will make viewing the slideshow even more fun and interesting for guests.

If you have photos that have not been formatted digitally— prints from other people, photos taken with film, or perhaps images from school yearbooks or newspaper clippings, you can either scan them into your computer or take a photo of the image with your digital camera and convert it that way. Photo specialty shops will also do it for you—for a fee.

Slideshow Projector and Screen

If you don't already have a projector and screen, they are relatively inexpensive on Amazon. Reviews are helpful. Any mini projector will work fine.

I included a description and link to the screen and stand we purchased for my daughter's Bat Mitzvah in the resources section at the back of this book. Altogether, we paid less than $70 for the screen and stand, and they did the job well.

Tip

There is nothing more frustrating than a tech glitch to derail your confidence the night of the celebration. Be sure to test the equipment out at home before going live at your event, and ask your venue about electrical outlets and suggested setup. You may also want to ask a tech-

savvy friend or family member attending the Bar or Bat Mitzvah to serve as standby tech support the night of the event.

Music

Music and dancing set the pace and the ambiance. Your DJ or bandleader will be integral to keeping the celebration moving and introducing people and activities, so choose someone whose approach to the celebration closely matches your desired effect.

Tip

If you are hosting an afternoon luncheon only, you may be able to save money by skipping the DJ and setting up a playlist instead.

However, if your event is in the evening, we can't stress enough the importance of hiring a professional.

Hire a Professional: Band or DJ?

There are two options to consider when choosing who will play music at your celebration—a DJ or a live band. While a DJ is more affordable, I highly recommend a live band if you can fit it in your budget. Our band even came with a DJ who could step in during breaks, maximizing the entertainment value of the evening.

Bands help create a special ambiance for a formal celebration. I find that a good band is well worth the money. When deciding where to save and where to splurge, this is an investment you may wish to consider. The energy and acoustics that a band creates are unique.

Any band that you consider should have from four to seven players, and prior experience handling Bar or Bat Mitzvahs. Be sure to ask for a resume of prior celebrations they have played, and check out the video footage on their website. Remember to watch the guests' faces and reactions as the band performs and interacts with the crowd.

We were very fortunate to have had access to top musical talent, as we live in Southern California. Our bandleader worked for Disney and Universal Studios and came to us highly recommended by a few hotels, so I knew he was going to be top notch.

Find a band that can play a variety of music and cover multiple genres, as you think about playing music that caters to every generation. It may help your bandleader or DJ if you share your "bucketed" guest list with them ahead of time, so they know and understand the age groups of your crowd.

Talk with your bandleader or DJ about music and song choices that engage every generation. When considering music selections, be sure to play a variety that caters to every generation to get people up and dancing! This is a teachable experience for your child since it sends the message to them that the Bar or Bat Mitzvah is to be shared with all of the people who attend the event, not just a select few. Be sure to play '60s and '70s music for baby boomers and '40s and '50s music for older generations.

We also included a great mix of generational songs at my daughter's Bat Mitzvah, as well as a handful of Broadway musical show tunes since her friends perform in a musical theatre group together. The sing-alongs were very special and will be remembered forever.

If you hire a band, make sure you've booked your venue for a good allotment of time in order to maximize the experience. Our reception ballroom was booked from six o'clock to midnight. While we were planning the event, six hours seemed like it would be too much time, but the celebration easily could have gone on longer!

If your venue charges a flat rate, make sure you negotiate the maximum amount of time permitted.

Turn Down the Volume

I can't urge this enough, but please keep the noise level down, especially when guests are socializing before and during dinner.

It is important that people don't feel overwhelmed by music that is blaring. Guests who feel overwhelmed or can't hear their conversations may withdraw and leave your party early.

Consider your guests' ears. Loud music can interfere with conversation and cause pain for guests of all ages, but especially for older guests or those with hearing impairments.

DJ music can be particularly noisy because of the high-pitched tones in electronic music.

Guests at your event will want to create connections and have meaningful interactions with others. Loud music prevents that from happening.

At one Bar Mitzvah we attended, the host provided earplugs. I thought it was a nice idea, but an even better idea is just to keep the music at a reasonable level. The louder the music does not mean the better the party.

Pro Tip: Headphones for Adults and Kids

Since our band included a DJ, whenever the band was on a break, the DJ would take over and play games with the teens and adults. He brought sixty illuminated headphones (see photo), which allowed him to play games and perform sing-alongs while the parents, family friends, and relatives enjoyed their dinner.

We could see the teens hopping around the table, laughing and having a great time, while the adults could converse with their friends at their table. It was a great modern twist on the celebration and helped ensure everyone had a great time. Another upside to the headphone idea is the noise factor. The kids could listen to music, but it didn't interfere with the adults' conversations.

If you decide to hire a DJ, you might want to ask if they offer a headphone option.

It made my daughter's Bat Mitzvah very special by adding an unexpected touch, and was absolutely loved by all guests. It was like a secret shared-group activity for the teens, and very entertaining for the adults to see modern technology.

Whatever you do, make sure the DJ that you hire comes with glowing referrals and recommendations. We have good friends who pulled off a fantastic Bat Mitzvah because their DJ was top notch. He was able to engage all of the guests and keep the noise at a decent level.

Dancing

Guests love to dance at a celebration. And those who don't dance will still enjoy watching friends and family on the dance floor! In Chapter 10, we talked about the size of your dance floor. Here, we introduce traditional and current dances that you may want to include at your Bar or Bat Mitzvah.

The *Hora* and Other Jewish Dances

Traditional Jewish dances like the *Hora* and *Hava Nagila* kick off a night of dancing. These dances and lifting the Bar or Bat Mitzvah on the chair may be one of the most well-known Jewish traditions. Your non-Jewish guests will have seen these dances on TV and in the movies and be very excited to witness them in person.

Expect close to full guest participation on the dance floor during these dances. Guests generally hold hands and circle around the Bar or Bat Mitzvah. These traditional dances can last anywhere from fifteen to twenty minutes.

Chair Lifting Tradition

Historically, only the Bar or Bat Mitzvah child was lifted in the chair, but the ritual is undergoing a shift in tradition. Nowadays, it is normal to see the child's parents and siblings lifted too.

We stuck with older traditions for my daughter's Bat Mitzvah and decided that we only wanted our Mitzvah child to be lifted.

Both methods are popular and perfectly acceptable, so if you (as the parent) want to be lifted, go for it!

As we were planning my daughter's Bat Mitzvah, our band-leader recommended that she be lifted on a chair with arms. The closest thing we could find at home was a beach chair. We took the beach chair to the celebration, but the moment we lifted her, we knew we had made a mistake. She started slipping and falling off in a reclined position.

We immediately swapped out the beach chair for a sturdier chair provided by the venue. Although it didn't have arms, the sturdy chair worked fine and everything turned out okay in the end.

Tip

Learn from our mistake! Don't use a chair that is flimsy or can fold up on your child, even if it has arms. Use a sturdy chair. If you can find one with arms, even better.

I recommend recruiting four large male guests to lift the chair in order to provide the most stable experience for the child and avoid mishaps.

After the *Hora* and other Jewish dances, the band or DJ might slip right into other music for guests to dance to, in an effort to keep people on the dance floor.

Expect about half of the dancers to sit down or grab a drink at this time, while the rest will stay and continue to dance.

Here are a few dances guaranteed to get people on the floor. The DJ or bandleader can play any of them during a lull to re-energize the dance floor, or just after the *Hora* and the Jewish dances, while everyone is already moving.

The Charleston

For your more seasoned guests, imagine the roaring '20s and all the glam of *The Great Gatsby*—flapper dresses and jewels and high kicking fun! The famous dance of the era was called the Charleston, which is easy to learn and has withstood the test of time. Teens and adults of all ages will love to dance the Charleston.

You can learn how to dance the Charleston on YouTube with a simple search. (Type in: "How to dance the Charleston from the 1920s.")

Once you've got it down, you can simplify the moves and have someone demonstrate for your guests. Let them know that having fun is the key, not getting the dance moves perfect! Talk with your bandleader or DJ ahead of time to let them know you'd like to do the Charleston. They'll be able to choose a song to complement the dance and may even bring along a dance specialist to do demonstrations.

Thriller

Teens will love learning this classic dance, created by Michael Jackson. It's a bit trickier than the Charleston, with a more complicated dance sequence, so you may want to choose someone in your family who is a gifted dancer or hire a professional dancer to come in and teach the moves.

Again, a quick search on YouTube for "how to dance the Thriller by Michael Jackson" will turn up a tutorial so that you can learn ahead of time.

Thriller is always danced to the song "Thriller" by Michael Jackson. Your teens—and guests who were teens in the '80s and '90s—will love to bust a move as soon as they hear the iconic opening beat.

The Cha-Cha Slide

This dance is always a hit! Teen and adult guests alike will be able to follow the moves, which are called out during the song, like instructions.

My preferred YouTube search term for this dance is "Mr. C The Slide Man, Cha-Cha Slide."

You will need to make sure the band knows the song or the DJ has the Mr. C song for the dance.

Tip

If you get a video release signed by your guests, this is a fun video to post on YouTube!

Hire a Dance Instructor

You may want to consider hiring a dance professional who specializes in teaching a specific type of dance. I mentioned a professional to teach Thriller, who might be great at teaching moves to famous pop songs and music videos.

Other dance pro options could include the Salsa, Waltz, Tango, Texas Two-Step, or the Rhumba.

If you are concerned that guests may be reluctant to approach the dance floor, a professional can energize the room and make everyone comfortable. People will enjoy the unique experience of learning new dances alongside other beginners, and your guests will feel more confident and engaged.

Entertainment for All Ages

Remember to refer back to Chapter 9 and your bucketed guests list as you consider where to invest your entertainment dollars. Look for entertainers who appeal to several age brackets to get the most out of your Mitzvah dollars.

The number of booths and activities you offer is completely up to you. Guests like something to do, but remember that the primary focus of the evening is not to host a carnival, but to acknowledge a religious celebration. Please do keep things tasteful.

Here are a small sampling of several options that will give guests something to do beyond the blessings, toasts, dinner, and dance floor:

- magicians,

- caricature artists,

- hat making,

- henna tattoo artists,

- jewelry making,

- photo booths,

- cell phone case designs.

Tip

If you're on a tight budget, I recommend that you choose entertainment that engages guests in longer activities. Hire vendors that provide entertainment for an ample time so that guests know that they will be available throughout the evening. That way guests won't feel rushed or like they have to wait in a long line to participate.

Some booths, such as photo booths, are naturally very quick, and guests are in and out in fifteen to twenty seconds. You'll get more bang for your entertainment buck if you focus on vendors with a longer entertainment time benefit.

Caricature Artists

Caricature artists are adored by guests of all ages, from small children through grandparents. Every generation can appreciate having their picture drawn, and a caricature is a nice keepsake.

Hat Makers

Hat makers are another wonderful option that can be enjoyed by every generation and result in a beautiful keepsake.

We noticed that every age group at my daughter's Bat Mitzvah took advantage of the hat-making booth, and it was so fun to see guests wear them on the dance floor and it was quote a hit.

Tip

By choosing arts and crafts vendors such as the caricature artists and hat maker, you've built in guest souvenirs and can avoid buying party favors!

Magicians

Magicians are great icebreakers, so I recommend booking them at the start of the celebration, during the cocktail hour. They relax guests as soon as they walk into the celebration, and adults and children are amused by their skill set.

If you do hire a magician, know that you only need to book them for a limited time. While other vendors will be booked for most of the night, once the celebration gets underway, new entertainment options will take the magician's place.

Games and Activities

In addition to entertainment provided by professional vendors, you and your band or DJ can plan fun games to play throughout the evening to keep everyone engaged.

The following games and activities can be coordinated in advance and sprinkled throughout the night to add variety. Ask your DJ or bandleader about additional ideas that we haven't considered.

One wonderful thing about these sorts of activities is that most of them don't cost anything extra—unless you want to throw in a gift, so they're budget-friendly. At the same time, they amp up the entertainment value and keep things interactive and focused on the guest experience.

Great for all ages, games are especially useful for keeping younger guests entertained and off their cell phones.

Centerpiece Giveaway Games

The first activity is more of a tradition than a game thrown in for entertainment. The centerpiece giveaway should occur before dinner instead of later on, in case guests need to leave early. There are many options for the centerpiece giveaway.

Pass the Money

This game is similar to musical chairs and we did this for my daughter's Bat Mitzvah. Each table had a single Monopoly bill hidden in the birdhouse. When it was time for the game, we told guests where to find the fake money.

Tip

Another fun twist is to have the teen tables scramble to ask their parents for a dollar to get the game started.

Once every table had the single bill ready to go, guests were instructed to pass the money around as the music played.

When the music stopped, our bandleader announced a twist! The guest to the left of the person holding the dollar won the centerpiece.

Left and Right Story

Have your Bar or Bat Mitzvah child announce story time for everyone. Begin by asking the youngest person at each table to pick up a spoon. Then tell everyone to listen very carefully to the story. Whenever they hear the word "right," they have to pass the spoon to the right. Every time they hear "left," they'll pass it to the left. At the end of the story whoever is holding the spoon will win the centerpiece.

We've included a sample story below that you can feel free to copy and take to the celebration if you choose this centerpiece giveaway game. The words left and right are capitalized to help you track when people are supposed to pass the spoon.

To avoid a page full of pronouns that look like s/he or his/her, we've written the story using a female pronoun. You should be able to switch it to he and his for a Bar Mitzvah without any problem. If the Bar or Bat Mitzvah will be the storyteller, substitute pronouns for I/my.

Sample Story:

"This morning, {Bar or Bat Mitzvah child's name} LEFT her house and was on her way to synagogue for the {Bar or Bat} Mitzvah.

But about halfway there, as she turned RIGHT, she remembered that she had LEFT her speech RIGHT by the door! She knew RIGHT away that she had to turn around and head RIGHT back home to get her speech.

So she turned RIGHT, then LEFT, and LEFT again, before finally turning RIGHT into her driveway.

Sure enough, there it was, RIGHT where she had LEFT it, RIGHT next to the door. Well, the {Bar or Bat} Mitzvah ceremony was lovely, wouldn't you agree? Nothing was LEFT out, and the speech was just beautiful.

So now there's nothing LEFT to say, except enjoy the rest of the evening.

Just for fun though, pass once more to the LEFT. Now, see… that was fun! RIGHT? The end. Congratulations, you just won the centerpiece!"

The person holding the spoon on the final right wins the centerpiece! Guests will pay very close attention to make sure the spoon gets passed around, and there are sure to be giggles throughout the game.

Let's Make a Deal

In Let's Make a Deal, the DJ or bandleader (or a guest or family member who is selected ahead of time and agrees to run games and make announcements) goes around to each table and asks for some obscure item, such as a mint, business card, emery board or old flip phone. Whoever comes up with the item first wins the centerpiece.

Sing-Alongs

I've found that many teenagers and younger kids love to participate in sing-alongs. They're fun, dramatic and silly. (It may have something to do with the fact that my Bat Mitzvah daughter is into musical theater, but all of her friends really enjoyed the activity!)

Our band engaged the teens in a sing-along while adults were socializing at dinner. They handed out lyrics of favorite songs so that everybody who wanted to participate would know the words.

Everyone enjoyed the experience very much and appreciated having the lyrics so it didn't matter how familiar they were with each word.

Popular family-friendly music from Disney films is great for a sing-along, as people of all ages from young children through grandparents will recognize it. The kids at my daughter's Bat

Mitzvah had a blast singing "Supercalifragilisticexpialido-cious" from *Mary Poppins* as one of their choices.

Trivia

All of our guests, from teens through adults, loved to partic-ipate in trivia. During dinner, while the band was on a break, the DJ would play music and ask guests which television show it came from.

It turned into a fun, friendly competition between teens and adults as guests would raise their hands and attempt to guess. Many guests said they enjoyed it very much.

Scavenger Hunt

Scavenger hunt can be played by as many or as few players as want to participate. It is catered to the kids and teens as it's a high-energy, active game, but adults can play too.

There is no way to work a cell phone and run around on a scavenger hunt! (You may have noticed by now that the key to a low-tech night is plenty to do!)

To start, have each player grab a chair, set it on the dance floor, and sit down. The DJ or bandleader will then call out an item that the players need to search for. When they find it, they return to the dance floor and sit down on any available chair.

The excitement builds as you remove one chair before the players come back. The person who does not have a chair to sit on when they get back is out. The play continues with new things to look for, while one chair disappears each time.

The first person to come back with the final item and sit down is your winner.

You may want to have a special gift ready to give to your winner. If you want to make it even more exciting for the teens, you can have three gifts—one each for first place, second place, and third place.

You can prepare for the game by hiding a wide variety of items around the room (e.g., specific finger food, a hidden coin in the centerpieces, specially colored balloons or menus taped underneath the tables), or you can have the DJ or bandleader call out things that are already in the room, such as a cocktail napkin or a spoon. (Just make sure that anything that belongs to the venue, such as a spoon, is not fragile and is returned to its rightful place.)

Pass the Gift

For this game, you'll need a nice small gift—something that would appeal to both boys and girls. Wrap the gift in several layers of paper. You can even layer in different size boxes as you're wrapping the gift to give the illusion of something much bigger. That adds a fun element of surprise.

Have participants form a circle on the dance floor, and ask your band or DJ to play an upbeat song. As the song is playing, players quickly pass the gift to the right and keep on passing. To keep it moving, you can tell them it's like a game of hot potato, and anyone who tries to hold the gift for too long is out!

When the music stops, the person holding the gift unwraps a layer. Then the music starts again and players continue passing the gift.

The guest who unwraps the last layer gets to keep the gift.

The anticipation and curiosity of how many layers of wrapping paper could be hiding the gift make it a lot of fun for everyone playing and watching.

Who Knows Best?

Prior to the celebration, write out fifteen to twenty trivia questions about your Bar or Bat Mitzvah's interests, hobbies, personal history and favorites (e.g., food, color, song, movie, etc.).

To play, seat your child on the far end of the dance floor with their back facing the guests. Gather as many players as want to play, and split people into five groups working together. The groups can be multi-generational. Make sure there is at least one child in each group.

As the DJ or bandleader asks trivia questions, teammates confer and discuss their answers. The youngest child from each group is invited to yell out the answer at any time, and the group that answers correctly first gets to move five steps closer to the Bar or Bat Mitzvah.

The group closest to your child when the last question is answered correctly wins! I advise a small gift for each child or adult in the winning group for their efforts.

Making Memories

Before we close out the book, I wanted to mention the importance of hiring a wonderful photographer and videographer to record the Bar or Bat Mitzvah and help remember the celebration for years to come.

Once you've read through what to look for in a photographer or videographer, be sure to read the bit about guest photos that follows. Posing for pictures with your guests is one more way to honor them and express your thanks for their participation.

Photographer and Videographer Selection

When selecting a photographer (highly recommended) and videographer (nice, but optional), spend time looking at their portfolios, and ask to speak with former clients if you can. Look at their stylistic approach to photography, and make sure it matches your wants and needs.

Does the photographer typically take mostly photos of the Bar or Bat Mitzvah (or the bride and groom if looking at a wedding portfolio) and their family, or are guests widely represented in photos? Is their portfolio primarily formal photos, carefully constructed scenes, or candid, or a mix? Is the style more artistic, journalistic, atmospheric, or portrait? Do they take photos of the details, such as centerpieces and other decorations, or is it primarily people? Do photos look like they've been heavily touched-up, or more natural? There are no right or wrong answers. It is simply a matter of personal preference.

How does the videographer edit the video? Might they include messages from guests to the Bar or Bat Mitzvah? What is the sound quality? How long is the video? Once you've shared the schedule of the evening, what is their plan for filming major moments? Does the contract include raw footage?

Take into careful consideration how many hours your photographer and videographer will cover the Bar or Bat Mitzvah celebration.

Tip

Our party lasted six hours and we had the photographer for the first three hours. In hindsight, not a lot happens in the first hour while cocktails are served, so if I had it to do over again, I might have moved the photographer schedule back a little bit.

If you don't plan to have a photographer stay for the full event, I recommend you schedule them to start taking pictures the last few minutes of the cocktail hour and then continue for about three to four hours.

If you're on a tight budget and need to squeeze the most out of every minute, share the event schedule with the photographer as early as possible and ask them to recommend the best hour or two to photograph.

Photo Deliverables

Negotiate photo deliverables—how and when you'll get your pictures—with your photographer.

Some photographers share all of the photos, while others provide only a selected few, generally based on a predetermined number of included images. Some upload pictures online or provide a flash drive or CD, and leave it up to you to print them. (If your computer has limited or no USB or CD access, this will be important to know ahead of time.) Others may give you a hardcover photo book of the event. Some photographers provide a slideshow on a disc.

I preferred to keep all photos taken at my daughter's Bat Mitz-vah, so I let the photographer borrow a hard drive I bought and he was able to load all of the photos onto it.

Don't gloss over they details while going through the con-tract. Ask exactly when and how photos will be delivered. You do not want there to be any surprises down the line.

Ask about uploading images to social media so that guests can view them. Do you need to use watermarked images or include photographer credit if you upload them to a platform like Facebook or once you have the photos, do ownership and photo usage rights transfer to you? Does the contract include a notice that the photographer can use images in their port-folio or marketing material, including public spaces online? Is that acceptable to you? It is worth noting that Facebook may have trouble uploading high-resolution files. Will your photographer provide lower resolution files for social media, or will you have to convert the images? It's simple enough to shrink the file size, but you'll want to learn how to do it ahead of time so that you're not frustrated once you've selected all of your favorite photos for upload and Facebook tells you the file is too large.

Video Deliverables

The same concepts apply when booking a videographer. Ask about what you should expect to receive in terms of film length and format, and be sure to provide a hard drive if you want all of the footage. Make sure all of these details are writ-ten into the contract.

Tip

For the budget conscious or for a special touch, in lieu of a videographer you can put signs in frames on every table requesting guests send their video clips they captured at the reception to your email address.

Guest Photos

At some point in the evening, be sure to honor your guests by taking photos with them. This ensures that you and your child personally greet everyone at the celebration, and makes a lovely keepsake for you and the guest.

The best time to make sure everyone is present and make sure you don't miss anyone is to take photos during dinner while guests are at their tables. Photos can be taken with the parents or just with the Bar or Bat Mitzvah child. Your family will visit all of the tables to avoid skipping any of your guests.

Work with the photographer to figure out the best way to coordinate and stage photos that don't end in dimly lit photos with half-eaten plates of food. The focus should be on the people, not the surroundings. Good pictures of decorations and food can be taken separately.

Guests will feel honored and excited to steal a moment with the host and hostess who took time out of their busy evening to be with them. Remember, anything that makes the guest feel special aligns with the message you want to convey.

Be sure to let guests know how they'll be able to view the photos at a later date, and then follow up when they're ready. You might want to add them to your Facebook or website page for easy viewing and accessibility

Party Wrap-Up

At the end of the night, and as people leave, be sure to thank them for coming, and express your appreciation for their presence in your Bar or Bat Mitzvah's life.

Then go home and pat yourself on the back for a job well done! You have built a memory for your child that will last a lifetime.

Parting Thoughts

Our goal by sharing our knowledge and experiences—good and bad—has been to support you on your path to creating a special day for all participants.

We want to make sure that your guests leave saying they felt welcomed, included, and honored for their presence, and had a lot of fun!

And we want to ease what can feel like an insurmountable task to plan and budget for the celebration by spreading it into a manageable schedule, giving you plenty of options on how to spend or save money.

We hope that you have felt our guidance and support throughout the book and learned something along the way.

Make sure your celebration maintains the spiritual connection that was emphasized at the ceremony and focus on your guests' experience when planning. These helpful tips will guide you toward having a successful Mitzvah!

Mazel Tov!!!

Appendices

Additional Resources

In addition to the resources and websites in this book, we recommend that you visit a Bar and Bat Mitzvah Expo, an event held in most major cities. Expos have all the connections and vendors that you need plan a fabulous Bar or Bat Mitzvah celebration, including entertainers, invitations, banquet facilities, photographers and videographers, party favors, clothing and much more—all under one roof!

Attending an Expo is the easiest way to get ideas, talk about celebration options, gather pricing information, and meet people face-to-face. Attending an Expo can save you several days of planning-related work, traveling to and fro, meetings, calling professionals, and searching the web. This is time well spent.

Of course, speak with your synagogue for all questions about your child's specific Bar or Bat Mitzvah ceremony.

In addition, we recommend you look into the websites that we mention throughout the book.

Websites and Emails Mentioned in the Book
(Listed By Chapter)

Chapter 2 **Charitable Organizations to Consider**

Holy Land Cats
www.holylandcats.wordpress.com
Contact: Anna Saul tovasaul@yahoo.com

Neve College for Women
www.nevey.org
Contact: Ellen Clyman: EllenClyman@nevey.org

World Animal Protection
  To learn more about Bear Sanctuaries:
    www.worldanimalprotection.us.org/bear-sanctuaries
  To donate: www.worldanimalprotection.us.org/ways-give

The Nature Conservancy
  www.nature.org

Additional Tikkun Olam Mitzvah Project Ideas

Mitzvah Bowl
  www.themitzvahbowl.com

Chapter 3 Bar and Bat Mitzvah Theme Ideas

Beaucoup
  www.beau-coup.com/bar-bat-mitzvah-theme-ideas.htm

Chapter 4 Date Estimate for Bar or Bat Mitzvah

Chabad
  www.chabad.org

Direct Date Calendar Link: www.chabad.org/calendar/
  bar-bat-mitzvah_cdo/aid/6227/jewish/BarBat-Mitz-
  vah-Date-Calculator.htm

Guest Room Hotel Blocks
  The Knot
  www.theknot.com/content/hotel-room-blocks-101

Kippot, Yarmulkes
  Mazel Skull Cap
  www.kippah.com

Party Favors
> Cool Party Favors
> www.cool-party-favors.com/bar-mitzvah-party-favors.html

Chapter 5 Frequently Asked Questions

My Jewish Learning
> www.myjewishlearning.com/article/what-a-barbat-mitzvah-guest-needs-to-know/

Chapter 7 Do-It-Yourself Innovations

Shutterfly
> www.shutterfly.com/cards-stationery/religious-celebrations/bar-bat-mitzvah-invitations

Personalized Mitzvah Website
> MyEvent
> mitzvahs.myevent.com

Do-It-Yourself Table Seating Place Cards
> Avery
> www.avery.com

Place Cards to Buy (paper/ cardstock)
> www.avery.com/products/cards/type/tent-~-place-cards

Place Card Templates
> www.avery.com/templates/category/cards?filters=-type1_Insertable%20Dividers,Tent%20%26%20Place%20Cards

Chapter 8 More Information about the Torah Reading

Hebcal
> www.hebcal.com

Weekly Torah Readings
> www.hebcal.com/sedrot/

Triennial Torah Reading Cycle
> www.hebcal.com/home/50/what-is-the-triennial-to-
> rah-reading-cycle

How to Chant the Torah Blessings
> YouTube (*transliterated into English*)
> youtu.be/kOEODiFstG0

Tikkun Olam Mitzvah Project
> For more information on the World Animal Protection
> website mentioned in the Sample Bat Mitzvah Speech,
> see link above, listed under Chapter 2.

Commentary Websites on the Weekly Parsha
> My Jewish Learning
> www.myjewishlearning.com

Hillel International
> hillel.org/jewish/archives

Navigating the Bible II: Online Bar/Bat Mitzvah Tutor
> bible.ort.org/books/torahd5.asp

Professional Speechwriter
> Ken Calof
> Contact: kcalof@gmail.com

Tzedekah Donations: Sanctuary Baskets and Arrangements
Mazon: A Jewish Response to Hunger
www.mazon.org

Chapter 11 Havdalah

My Jewish Learning
www.myjewishlearning.com/article/havdalah-taking-leave-of-shabbat

Bar or Bat Mitzvah Centerpiece Ideas
Pinterest
www.pinterest.com/mitzvahmagic/bar-mitzvah-centerpieces-diy/

Candle Lighting Ceremony Songs
Google
www.google.com
Search: "Candle Lighting Songs"

Portable Projector, Stand for Slideshow
Amazon
(VIVO 84" Portable Indoor Outdoor Projector Screen, 84 Inch Diagonal Projection HD 4:3 Projection Pull Up Foldable Stand Tripod on Amazon: approx. $70)
www.amazon.com/VIVO-Portable-Projector-Diagonal-Projection/dp/B00MR5SGBQ

Group Dances

YouTube

www.youtube.com

Search Terms:

"How to Dance the Hora"

"How to Dance the Hava Nagila"

"How to Dance the Charleston"

"How to Dance Thriller"

"How to Dance the Cha-Cha Slide"

Like This Book?

Please leave us a review on Amazon! We depend on you to spread the word and help other families plan their best Bar or Bat Mitzvah, one that will be remembered forever as a special and heartfelt memory.

Timeline Checklist

24 Months Before the Event

- ☐ Lock in Your Date
- ☐ Ask About Synagogue/Temple Requirements
- ☐ Enroll Child in Bar/Bat Mitzvah Preparation
- ☐ Estimate Number of Guests
- ☐ Determine Budget and Event Parameters (Day, Evening, Formal, Luncheon, etc.)
- ☐ Book a Venue

18 Months Before the Event

- ☐ Research and Select: Band, DJ, Photographer, Videographer, Florist, Entertainers
- ☐ Research, Interview, Select Caterer(s)
- ☐ Consider Hiring an Event Planner

12 Months Before the Event

- ☐ Choose Hotel(s) for Out-of-Town Guests
- ☐ Support Bar/Bat Mitzvah's Torah Studies and Check on Progress
- ☐ Begin Work on Custom Centerpieces, Flowers and/or Balloon Decorations
- ☐ Plan Invitations
- ☐ Mail Save the Date Cards

☐ Order *Tallit*, *Kippot*

☐ Plan Theme (*optional*)

☐ Book Tables for Additional Meals (e.g., Sunday Brunch)

6 Months Before the Event

☐ Select Guest Book or Sign-In Board (*optional*)

☐ Order Party Favors (*optional*)

☐ Write Parent and Teen Speeches

☐ Work on Celebration Slideshow (*optional*)

☐ Start Shopping for Clothes

3 Months Before the Event

☐ Finalize Guest List and Confirm Missing Addresses for Invitations

☐ Plan Table Seating

☐ Finalize Catering Menu for Celebration

☐ Select Hotel Room Gifts for Out-of-Town Guests (*optional*)

☐ Write a Song Playlist: Include Songs for Candle Lighting Ceremony

☐ Select Honorees for *Aliyot*, Torah Tasks, and Gift Presentations

☐ Make Hair Stylist, Pedicure, Manicure Appointments

1–2 Months Before the Event

☐ Mail Invitations (*6 Weeks Out*)

☐ Confirm RSVPs (*3 Weeks Out*)

☐ Confirm Date, Time, Schedule with All Vendors

☐ Guest List for Candle Lighting Ceremony (*optional*)

☐ Order Food for *Oneg Shabbat* and *Kiddush* luncheon

☐ Confirm and Complete Decorations

1 Week Before the Event

☐ Finalize Day-of-Event Schedule

☐ Make Checklist of Items to Take to Ceremony and Celebration

☐ Send Final Headcount to Caterer

☐ Finalize Seating Arrangements

☐ Hair, Manicure, Pedicure Appointments

☐ Formal Photos (*optional*)

☐ Confirm Sunday Brunch Reservations (*if hosting brunch*)

☐ Arrange Transportation for Out-of-Town Guests (*optional*)

☐ Drop off Hotel Guest Gift Bags (*optional*)

Index

Acknowledgements

Many people have helped make this book a reality.

First of all, I would like to thank Rabbi Mark Siedler and Lynetta Avery for their collaboration on the book. Mark's expertise in the area of Jewish knowledge was invaluable. Both he and Lynetta were instrumental in critical decisions that involved titles and subtitles, content and marketing. Lynetta was diligent at collecting information and researching all things related to B'nai Mitzvot. They both provided vital insights that were indispensable to me. I am grateful to have had the opportunity to work with them closely and I immensely enjoyed the experience.

I also want to thank Alana Garrigues for her unequivocal knowledge of book editing. She was instrumental at providing valuable comments not only regarding editing, but with all elements related to book development. She goes above and beyond an editor's tasks and provides valuable feedback regarding tasks related to successfully creating a book from start to finish. Her expertise and insights surpass the normal duties of an editor. Her dedication and love for editing makes her top notch and she was essential in the process of creating this book.

Thanks to Rabbi Brian Schuldenfrei for taking time out of his busy day to write the foreword for the book and providing insight and feedback. He stands out as an inspiration for both congregants and the community.

Thanks to Jessica Richardson for the outstanding book cover design! She is truly amazing!

Thanks to Chris Osman for the print and digital formatting, and for taking care of the technical side of laying out a book.

Lastly, I would like to thank all my friends who provided valuable information for the book. Thank you for sharing Bar and Bat Mitzvah experiences with me. Their experiences highlighted the importance of planning a Mitzvah with all guests in mind.

About the Author and Contributors

Author Wendy Weber studied abroad in Israel for three years, and earned a Bachelor of Arts degree in Hebrew and Judaic Studies. Wendy currently lives in California with her family where she works as a Data Report Analyst. She hopes this book provided you with valuable information that she uncovered during the planning stages of her daughter's Bat Mitzvah.

Rabbi Mark Siedler obtained his Rabbinical Degree from the Jewish Theological Seminary (JTS) in New York, by studying for eight years at various Jewish Institutions in Jerusalem, Los Angeles, and New York. He also has a joint master's degree in Education from JTS and Teachers College Columbia University.

Rabbi Mark and **Lynetta Avery** are married spiritual life coaches. They have been lifelong spiritual students sharing their knowledge of spiritual practices with their clients. They guide people into a new understanding of life's challenging experiences to find better health, wealth, inner peace and love from their coaching.

Rabbi Brian Schuldenfrei served for seven years at Sinai Temple in Los Angeles under Rabbi David Wolpe. He also sat on the Rabbinical Assembly's Resolutions Committee, the Rabbinic Cabinet of the Masorti Foundation for Conservative Judaism, the United Jewish Community's Young Leadership Cabinet, and the Executive Board of the Miami Rabbinic Association. He received his B.A. with honors from Washington University in St. Louis.

Rabbi Schuldenfrei was a distinguished student at The Jewish Theological Seminary, the school of his rabbinic ordination. While studying for ordination, Rabbi Schuldenfrei served as the rabbinic intern for the New York Board of Rabbis Center for Spiritual Care, Beit T'Shuvah, a Jewish recovery center in Los Angeles, and The National Center for Learning and Leadership (CLAL).

Made in the USA
Middletown, DE
12 December 2019